Flyfishing for TROUT A TO Z

Mike Faw

Stoeger Publishing Company ◆ Accokeek, Maryland

Stoeger Publishing®
Great Outdoor Books & More Since 1924

STOEGER PUBLISHING COMPANY IS A DIVISION OF BENELLI U.S.A.

BENELLI U.S.A.
Vice President and General Manager:
  Stephen Otway
Vice President of Marketing and Communications:
  Stephen McKelvain

STOEGER PUBLISHING COMPANY
President: Jeffrey Reh
Publisher: Jay Langston
Managing Editor: Harris J. Andrews
Design & Production Director:
  Cynthia T. Richardson
Photography Director: Alex Bowers
Imaging Specialist: William Graves
National Sales Manager: Jennifer Thomas
Special Accounts Manager: Julie Brownlee
Editorial Assistant: Christine Lawton
Administrative Assistant: Shannon McWilliams
Illustration: William Graves
Proofreader: Celia Beattie

Published by Stoeger Publishing Company
17603 Indian Head Highway, Suite 200
Accokeek, Maryland 20607

BK0311
ISBN: 0-88317-255-0

Library of Congress Control Number: 2002110073

Manufactured in the United States of America.

Distributed to the book trade and
to the sporting goods trade by:
Stoeger Industries
17603 Indian Head Highway, Suite 200
Accokeek, Maryland 20607
301-283-6300 Fax: 301-283-6986
www.stoegerindustries.com

OTHER PUBLICATIONS:

PHOTOGRAPHY CREDITS
Bill Buckley/The Green Agency: *Cover and title page;*
Duane Raver/USFWS: 5, 86, 88, 89;
Courtesy of The American Museum of Fly Fishing: 10;
Donnie Sexton/Travel Montana: 54

Table of Contents

Introduction: To Wild Places and the Trout that Live There

When it comes to wild encounters, nothing compares with pulling a wildly splashing, determined trout from a cold mountain stream and staring into its eyes. While you have it in hand is also a good time to admire its brilliant colors, graceful form and many unique features. Then it's time to gently let that gem of a fish slip back into its underwater world to live and hopefully grace you with another bite on a future date.

I have been a fortunate angler. My travels with a flyrod have taken me from cold Blue Ridge Mountain headwaters in western North Carolina to the wilds of Alaska, and from northern California to the backcountry of Maine in my pursuit and admiration of trout. From in-stream wading, to float-tubing a high country lake, to fly-in plane trips to remote backcountry lakes, one common thread stands out among all of my trips: Trout. Trout live in some of North America's most scenic areas, and I have been fortunate to go there and cast a flyrod.

Along the streams I've met—and

fished with—anglers that lived to fish, and others that simply enjoyed occasionally pursuing trout or using a flyrod. Most of the anglers that had icy cold, trout-like blood running through their vanes did more that cast a flyrod in their pursuits. They also tied flies, built rods, took far-away trips, were active members in conservation organizations, and introduced others to the fine art of fly-fishing for trout.

In recent years my focus has been more on going to and experiencing a region rather than simply catching trout. There's just something about the wild places where trout live that beckons some folks. The experience and memories put an odd sparkle in every visitor's eyes. When talk of the outdoors and fishing fades to trout fishing, you can see that sparkle in every enthusiast's eyes. Their smiles widen, they relax more, and you can tell that they'd rather be in the stream with a flyrod in hand rather than where they are now. I share their thoughts, but like them, I am trapped in that vicious cycle of working to earn money so I can go fly-fishing.

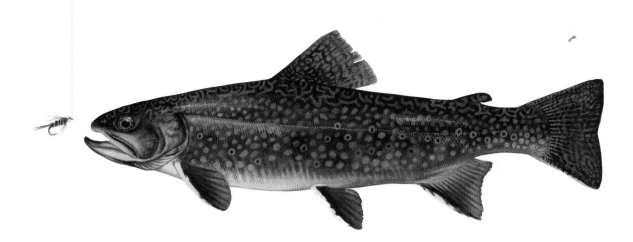

In recent years, I've seen that sparkle-in-the-eye caused by a splash of cold mountain water and the tug of a trout on a tight flyline in Reuth, my wife's, eyes. I'd like to extend a sincere thanks to her for willingly going along on many recent fishing expeditions, and for making many of them a great success and pleasure.

If you like fly-fishing for trout, you owe it to yourself to introduce someone else to this life-enriching endeavor. The trout need all the support they can get, and so do the wild places they call home.

—*Michael D. Faw*

Acknowledgement

I have been fortunate to cross the path of Captain George Weise from Patterson, North Carolina, as part of an after-school fly-tying program. Mr. Weise could tie flies with great skill and in such fine detail that you'd think the insect would fly away when the vice was loosened. He could also cast that tiny fly across a basketball court and drop it into your shoe. He was even more impressive to watch—and fish with—on a river. I owe my background basics in much of my fly fishing knowledge to his enthusiastic introduction and ongoing encouragement.

*The author's wife, Reuth, flyfishing in the Appalachian Mountains
in western North Carolina.*

1 A Background in the Fine Art of Flyfishing

ADAMS

(Dry Fly)
Popular Sizes:
10, 12, 14, 16, 18, 20, 22
Hook Type:
Extra-fine dry fly.
Bigeye in smaller sizes.
Thread:
Black 8/0
Tail:
Brown and grizzly
hackle fibers
Body:
Muskrat or medium
gray dubbing
Wing:
Grizzly hackle tips—
upright and divided
Hackle:
Brown & grizzly, mixed

In the beginning—angling with a pole and line was documented in ancient Egypt by crude drawings discovered there, and those sketches are possibly the first recorded angling information where a rod was involved. I seriously doubt that the Egyptians were flyfishing, but the use of a fishing rod by humans was well underway. While man's use of tools, in this case a rod, was obviously advancing, this was not fly fishing.

Centuries later the question arose from an astute angler: How do I cast a small lightweight lure that looks like a small, nearly microscopic insect out any distance to trick and catch a trout? Through the experimentation process, it was determined that the rod needed to be whiplike and able to propel a very lightweight lure—the fly—out across the water and gently drop it to the water surface in a manner to trick a trout. This meant moving the line and fly gingerly and not creating any unnecessary or unnatural ripples. The flyfishing process was underway, but who thought of the process first is still uncertain.

History heaps much of the credit on Europeans as the early inventors of the equipment and processes for flyfishing for trout. The early European angling period—well before America was discovered—saw anglers using wooden rods of sometimes gigantic lengths up to 20 feet long to cast flies. These early rods were crafted from numerous species of trees found in the countryside. The flies that they cast were a blend of many common materials, including dog and bear hair, and the feathers of various fowl tied to hooks. In recent years, however, there have been rumblings in the flyfishing world that the anglers in Austria and Germany could have gotten the jump on the English and invented flyfishing equipment and the popular technique. All of this speculation about yesteryear's anglers, and who were the first true fly fishers, generates great chatter around today's campfires and in dark, smoke-filled lodge dens late at night after the sun has set and the fish tales grow larger. When Europeans discovered America, however, and came across the Atlantic, flyfishing came with them.

I like to believe that early American settlers had a fly rod tucked away in their private possessions on the

The author fly-fishing for trout in an Appalachian tailwater.

An icon of a Western fly fisherman, this statue meets visitors at the Bozeman, Montana, airport.

ships as they crossed the ocean. The die-hard anglers who forgot their fly rods set about making a new one shortly after they came aground in the New World.

Those early American anglers came aground in search of places to cast and fish to catch along with their pursuit of other freedoms. Much of the fishable waters in the Old World were privately owned and controlled by the landowner. America was created with public waterways and public trout fishing waters remain common today.

The search in the New World for more unspoiled waters, bigger trout and scenic rivers led settlers into the Appalachians, down the westward side, across the Midwest and on to the Rockies. As covered wagons pushed west, I believe the old hinged trunks which held the family's treasures also had a small leather pouch with a few flies tucked inside. Somewhere in some of those trunks were fly rods. Could the earliest rush to California have actually been caused by a big trout? If you've fished any of the great trout waters in California, you'll pause and ponder the possibilities.

Sometime after the early American exploring was complete, those settlers who built a log home and were prospering did what all folks have done since the early days—they went flyfishing. Forget the 20-foot English rods, gaudy flies and other Old World ways. American violin crafters began splicing together small slivers of wood and bamboo to create fine rods—or instruments—for flyfishing that matched the demands and tastes of anglers in the New World. Our world and the fine sport of fly fishing has never quite been the same.

Flyfishing as we know it took on a uniquely American flare that worked well in our nation's waters, used our nation's fur and feather resources, and created the history we call fly fishing today. Fortunately for us this history has been well recorded and much of the early American era memorabilia is tucked away in museums around the nation. If you want to see important parts of America's fly-fishing heritage, there are several first-class museums for you to visit. Take a tour in the American Museum of Fly Fishing in Manchester, Vermont, and you'll see much of how our flyfishing era began, and be amazed how far we've come in the past 200 years. This museum has a most impressive display of flies and old reels. A hint for visitors: Take your fly rod. The famed Battenkill River is just down the hill and within walking distance of this museum. The museum is located near the Orvis showroom.

While today's technology propels flyfishing forward with new rod

The Orvis shop in Manchester, Vermont, offers fishing clinics and rental gear.

A Cabela's store is a first stop for many fly anglers wanting to gear up with rods, waders, or flies. The staff can point you to local waters and tell you what the fish are biting.

Dan Bailey's fly shop in Livingston, Montana, is one of the West's premier angling destinations and a must for anyone heading to the Yellowstone region.

These antique flies and reels and the rare publications pictured below are some of the early American flyfishing gear displayed at the American Museum of Fly Fishing in Manchester, Vermont.

materials, large arbor reels, breathable waders and other space-age niceties, there are those who work to preserve the past. They still tie the old patterns, such as the gray hackle from the Appalachian region, and a special breed of die-hard anglers still shape and glue bamboo to create masterpiece rods. Flyfishing often becomes what you make of it.

If you want to see a unique collection of angling history, you owe it to yourself to visit another fishing museum, like the National Fresh Water Fishing Hall of Fame. This museum is located inside of a huge fish-shaped building in Hayward, Wisconsin. You can look at many

aspects of the sport of flyfishing during yesteryear, or climb to the museum's second floor observation deck and stand inside the fish's mouth to look out across Hayward. This museum displays the rods and reels possibly used by your grandfather or great-grandfather. A hint for visitors: The famed Brule River is a short drive away. Take your fly rod and try to catch a rainbow, brown, brook or steelhead on the Brule. The river also has occasional salmon runs out of Lake Superior.

Flyfishing has always played an important part in America's outdoor recreation pursuits. Honorable anglers like Lee Wulff, Cap Weise, Izaak Walton, and Curt Gowdy on the *American Sportsman* television series have inspired others to make that first addicting cast. Western rivers full of fly fishers on a weekend morning and the number of specialty fly shops around the nation, many located well away from trout waters, attest to the strong public interest in flyfishing. What does the future hold?

All serious fly fishers should go to a local fly shop and marvel at where flyfishing is going. You'll see specialty lights for night fishing, release aids to remove hooks from fish, synthetic materials for fly bodies and a large assortment of books and videos. Fly angling history is further expanded each year in America by Trout Unlimited chapters teaching youngsters about flyfishing, or by the Federation of Fly Fishermen holding their annual get-together where new fly patterns emerge and cutting-edge casting theories are introduced. A hint for anglers: The FFF's International Fly Fishing Center is located in Livingston, Montana, near the famed Yellowstone River. Many world-class fly shops, like Dan Bailey's, are nearby and can tell you the most productive fly for anglers at the time of your visit. Take a fly rod and try catching trout in town or go upstream to Yellowstone Park.

Numerous fishing tackle shows and events—such as trade shows and sportsmen's conventions—held around the year introduce new products and new trends to fly anglers everywhere. These shows are held coast to coast so you should be able to find one within a day's drive of your location. Part of the fun in flyfishing is exploring the new gear that emerges each season. If you are interested in a

particular product that you see somewhere or read about in a magazine, try contacting the manufacturer and see if you can attend a seminar or meeting where their sales representative will be previewing the product in your area.

In between your trips to learn about flyfishing, you should grab a fly rod and do some casting and fishing. Our nation is blessed with numerous rivers, lakes and small mountain streams where we can pursue trout. I sincerely hope that along your journey in life and flyfishing that you catch—and release—a trout.

BEADHEAD EMERGING SPARKLE CADDIS

(Nymph)
Popular Sizes: *12, 14, 16*
Hook Type: *2 X long nymph*
Thread: *Olive 6/0*
Tail: *Section of Antron shuck left hanging over rear.*
Abdomen: *Olive dubbing with cream Antron yarn shuck.*
Thorax: *Peacock herl*
Legs: *Brown partridge fibers*
Head: *Brass bead*

EXPLORING FLYFISHING HISTORY

If you are seeking a place to further explore the history of flyfishing—from rods and reels to fly patterns and tackle boxes—visit one or all of these museums. Many are located near famed trout waters, so bring along your fly rod and gear and go flyfishing after your tour.

American Museum of Fly Fishing
Manchester, Vermont
(802) 362-3300
www.amff.com

Catskill Fly Fishing Center and Museum
Livingston Manor, New York
(914) 439-4810

International Fly Fishing Center
Livingston, Montana
(406) 222-9369

National Fresh Water Fishing Hall of Fame
Hayward, Wisconsin
(715) 634-4440

*Bamboo fly rods, such as the one shown above, are usually made of six triangle-shaped
strips of "Tonkin cane" glued together to form the hexagonal shaft of the rod.*

2 | *Fly Rods*

**BEADHEAD
PHEASANT TAIL**

(Nymph)
Popular Sizes:
14, 16, 18
Hook Type:
*Short-shank curved
nymph.*
Thread:
Brown 6/0 or 8/0
Tail:
*4-8 fibers ringneck
pheasant tail fibers.*
Body:
*Ringneck pheasant tail
fibers*
Ribbing:
Copper wire
Head:
Copper bead

The fly rod that you select will be the single most important decision that you'll make in your flyfishing career. Choose wisely and you'll have hours of fun, success and thrills. Choose poorly and you could have epic periods of frustration. The duty of a fly rod is to help you manage and propel fly line—and the fly at the end of a length of leader and tippet—to a precise location on the water near you. A fly rod helps you accomplish this through design and flexibility. The rod also helps you set the hook once a trout has graced you by the honor of accepting your offered fly. In the end, your fly rod will help you control and possibly land a trout if you hook one. Just remember that all successful angling involves the meeting of luck and skill. You'll be more skillful if you have the right fly rod in your hand.

So, which rod is the right one for you? Well, it all depends … when you decide that it's time to take the plunge and buy a fly rod, you need to first be honest with yourself. Where will you be fishing, what type of fly will you be casting and what species and size of fish do you plan to catch? Forget about dream fishing trips if this will be your first

fly rod purchase. You're searching for the right rod to help you gain the basics of casting and fly-fishing on your local waters as you learn how to flyfish. If you must, take a piece of paper and pen and write out an analysis of the flyfishing opportunities in your area, your current casting skill level and your angling goals. This information can help anyone—beginner or advanced—select the rod best suited for their needs.

Most fly anglers spend 95 percent of the time that they fish for trout on water that's within a one- or two-hour drive from their home. If this will be the case with you, then go to the waters where you'll be casting and size up the water conditions. The fabled limestone Pennsylvania trout rivers are much different in width and layout than the narrow, laurel-choked brook trout streams high in the southern Appalachians of western North Carolina. And those chilled, sparkling waters are far different in size, shape and depth than Montana's wide, open rivers. The Rocky Mountain state's trout waters are different from the trout-filled tailwaters and lakes near Redding, California. Waters in North

over which you'll be casting. The insects and other food sources in the water will dictate what size of fly you might be casting. The width of the water—from bank to bank—helps you determine what length of rod will be manageable there. Be honest with yourself about the width of the streams that you'll fish most often and you're off to a great start in selecting a fly rod.

Next, you'll need to honestly assess the size and type of trout you'll be likely to catch. While Hazel Creek in the Great Smoky Mountains National Park, for example, is not a trophy-class water and every pool does not harbor a 20-inch-plus trout (OK, some pools do!), large fish are sometimes caught there. You'll need to consider the possibilities of what size of fish you might encounter and choose a rod with the correct strength and weight to help you control and land that fish.

Contact the state game and fish department where you'll be fishing to learn about the state's designated trout waters, species of trout, state record fish and seasons, if applicable. Some states have pamphlets and map books to aid you in your assessment of the trout waters and your angling opportunities. You can readily find this information on many departments of natural resources (DNR) Web sites today.

Graphite (carbon fiber) fly rods, introduced in the 1960s, are both lightweight and strong and are the most popular rods used by today's fly anglers. A good tackle store can help you select the proper reel to match your choice of fly rod.

America that hold trout exist as far south as Texas and as far to the north in the remote reaches of Quebec, and each presents a unique angling experience and challenge. Which type of water do you live near and which stream, river or lake will you fish most often? Fly rods tend to be semi-specialized and no single rod will do it all and be perfect in any condition that you might encounter.

Your rod has to match the waters

Selecting a Rod

Rods are categorized by length and weight classification. Length is the total length of the rod when correctly assembled from the butt to the tip. A rod's weight is the manufacturer's recommended fly line weight for use while fishing with the rod and not the physical weight of the rod itself. Some rod manufacturers do include the rod's actual weight and some anglers find this information useful. You'll be able to determine the rod's characteristics by reading the specifications—a series of numbers and letters—found on the shaft and in front of the grip. For example, "Length 9'- Wt. 3⅛ oz.- 5 wt. Line" reveals that this rod is 9 feet long when assembled, weighs 3⅛ ounces without a reel attached and a 5-weight fly line

is recommended when fishing with the rod. You might see the manufacturer's name and model details included in the writing on some rods.

Nine-foot fly rods are the standard today and the most popular length with fly fishers. The most common weights—5 and 6—means that the rod is designed to handle fly lines falling within this standard classification. Fly rods are designed and designated with line-weight sizes ranging from 1 through 9 and the manufacturer recommends that the angler use a specific size of fly line with the rod. This weight line should make the rod perform as intended by the manufacturer. Again, these numbers have no bearing on the actual weight of the fly rod itself. Keep in mind that the fly line carries the fly out to the fish when you cast.

TIP:

As a Matter of Fact

To help keep your rod and reel clean while you are rigging up or disassembling your equipment at the end of a fishing adventure, just remove the floor mat from the vehicle and place it on the ground. This will prevent gravel and sand from damaging your rod, reel and fly line. Never leave the end of your rod sticking through an open vehicle door. An unexpected wind could slam the door and end your trip before it starts.

PARTS OF A FLY ROD

BUTT   REEL LOCK   REEL SEAT   GRIP   HOOK KEEPER

TIP   SNAKE GUIDE

STEPS TO FLY ROD SELECTION

If you can answer these questions, you're ready to buy a fly rod:

- Where will you be fishing and how would you describe the water?
- What fish species will you be fishing for and how big is the average fish?
- How will you be fishing the waters? Wading vs. float tube, casting upstream vs. downstream, etc.
- Will you take a small floatplane to reach the water?
- How much do you want to spend?

Write the answers down before you go into a store and you just might exit with a fly rod that meets your needs.

Should you select an 8-foot, two-piece or get an 11-foot, four-piece rod? Let the water and the fish you'll find there be your guides.

Most anglers will be well served by a 9-foot rod in 5-, 6- or 7-weight. Today these rods are recognized as the standard, based on their popularity, and anything that deviates too far from the norm up and down the scale is relegated to the status of specialty rod. The smaller the line weight number, the smaller in diameter and weight-per-foot the fly line will be. Small line weight numbers can also indicate that the rod will be more fragile. Smaller weight rods are better designed to cast small flies such as a minuscule #22 Trico. It's a thrill to land a big trout with a small weight line, and it takes a lot of finesse. A downside is that small rods and lightweight lines are more difficult to cast under windy conditions.

There has been some interest in recent years in fishing 1- and 2-weight rods. These rods can be expensive and are easily damaged. While I would not recommend one of these for a beginner, I could say that an experienced angler with one of these lightweight rods could

have a great day on the water under the right conditions.

On the upper end of the scale, you might want to buy—or rent—an 8-weight rod if you're headed to Alaska's King Salmon area to take on the 30-inch rainbows that thrive in the rivers there. I find that some heavier weight rods cast like concrete-reinforcing rebar, but any fly rod needs serious backbone when you're winching in those big Alaska trout that gobble dead salmon for lunch. These heavy-weight specialty rods are designed to use heavyweight fly lines and cast large flies. For example, the flesh fly that is popular in Alaska looks very similar in color, size and shape to a lucky rabbit's foot charm. It takes a strong, stiff rod with correctly matched fly line to propel this lure through the air and onto the water, especially when the flesh fly is wet. And the heavy-weight rod is also more manage-able in Alaska's robust winds.

A good rule of thumb is to buy lightweight and heavier rods as you become more experienced or more specialized in your fishing pursuits. In the beginning, rods in weights 5 to 7 are the best choices for most anglers.

The manufacturer or builder's choice of material for the rod's spine determines a rod's flex. You can identify a rod's spine—the stiffest and strongest side—by carefully pressing the rod's tip against the floor and gently rolling your

WHAT WEIGHT AND LENGTH?

In fly-fishing, the weight of the line and rod should always match because it is the line that carries the lure to the trout. In standard spinning rod and bait casting rigs, the weight of the lure pulls the monofilament line along as it zips through the air when cast.

WHEN FISHING

in small streams & creeks   small trout   1- to 3-weight rod with some flexing along the entire length of the rod from the handle to the tip would be a good choice for experienced anglers.

TO LAND MEDIUM-SIZED TROUT

10" to 20" long trout   8'- or 8½' rod   4- or 5- weight

PURSUING TROUT

in small to large rivers   rods in the 3- to 6-weight range with less flex (with the rod only bending forward of the half-length point) would be a good choice. You could safely fish small and medium sized flies with this rod.

PURSUING LARGE TROUT

on wide, open rivers & lakes (in the West and Rocky Mountains) 9-foot rod in 5- to 7-weight
that flexes in the forward section of the rod would be a good selection. You could cast large flies safely since the line flies on a higher plane and you are less likely to be hooked. Heavier lines also help to combat the high winds that are common in popular fly-fishing destinations like Montana. What is more, there are big insects in the western states, such as the famed stone flies, and it takes a heavier line and heavier rod to move large lures that match the hatch through the air and out to hungry trout.

palm across the rod. You'll notice a stiff side that resists bending, while another side of the rod will bend with ease. The spine should be opposite the eyes and helps the rod load under stress while performing like to a whip to propel the line and your fly through the air. A less flexible rod is known for making tight casts with small loops, and for quickly lifting fly line off the water's surface. Today this flex is called action with fast, medium and slow being the standards. There are no real industry standards here so you'll have to be the judge about what seems appealing to you.

Fast-action rods are stiff and flex only near the tip of the rod. Medium-action rods normally flex over the upper half or forward 60 percent of a rod. Slow-action rods flex from the tip to just forward of

the rod's grip on the thickest part of the shaft or nearly 90 percent of the rod bends. The choice when making a selection is based on your personal preference. If in doubt, go with a medium-action fly rod. The decision will become easier if you place a reel with line on the rod and try casting it on a grassy area, or better yet, on water near the store. Most fly shops will let you rig up a rod and try it before you buy. If the shop where you are considering a rod will not let you test it, move on to another shop. Would you buy a car without driving it?

Length Does Matter

Next, there's the question of length to consider when purchasing and using fly rods. While 9

the drift boats also like the extra clearance provided by the longer rods to avoid being hooked on windy days.

Moving down the length scale, I will sometimes drop to an 8-foot rod in summer in the Midwest when lush, green brush sprawls across the region's medium-sized rivers. I also go down to a 4-weight rod to precision cast #28 Tricos early in the morning on hot summer days. Again, choose a rod based on the river and waters where you'll spend most of your angling time and you'll be happy. As you will soon discover, no rod can be expected to do it all and cover all situations. As you expand your fishing areas and interests, you'll be inclined to own and use more than one fly rod.

This is great news for manufacturers and fly shops, but becomes a dilemma for anglers. You'll have to decide which rod—or rods—to use. Most fly fishermen on a trip now pack along at least two rods.

Many manufacturers take the guesswork out of outfit selection by offering complete packages that include rod, reel, backing, fly line and case. Scientific Anglers offers this ready-to-fish set in 5-, 6- and 8-weight rods.

feet has become the standard rod length of choice, and these rods are generally easy to maneuver and provide needed reach in open areas, their length can be a problem and burden in tight stream situations. In some western states in recent years, drift boaters and anglers who hop into tubes and fish trout-filled lakes have begun casting 9½- or 10-foot rods because they have lots of open water to cast over. Many guides in

The Human Factor

In addition to the weight and length, another frequently overlooked factor comes into play— human dexterity. Some anglers can pick up a rod and be skillfully casting in a short time, while others are

A MATCH OF FLY LINE AND FLY

The size of the fly that you intend to cast most of the time can also help determine the rod line and weight that you'll need. Here are the suggested matches:

Line and Rod Weight	Fly Sizes
3	28-12
4	26-10
5	24-8
6	20-6
7	16-4
8	12-1/0

not as graceful and might take weeks, months or years to become proficient. The upside to this factor is that it's an excuse for you to go fishing more often. The more you practice and fish, the better you become at casting and using a rod. The more you understand about flyfishing, the better you will become at selecting a rod to meet your preferences. No two humans are alike — that's why you'll find hundreds of rod options in an average fly shop. Somewhere the right rod is waiting for you.

When you decide to buy a rod or upgrade to a new rod, you'll find that there are manufacturers' catalogs, Web sites and fly shops that can help you find the perfect fly rod. Remember that just because your friend or dad has a particular rod does not mean that's the type for you. Most fly shops will rig up a rod and let you cast it. This is the only true way to test a rod. The worst thing you can do is pick up a rod from the rack, shake it a few times and watch the tip wiggle, and then buy it. When selecting a rod, you'll want to attach a reel loaded with line so that you can see how the total package goes together—and feels in your hand—before you open your wallet. Does it feel balanced? It should.

Get a Grip

When selecting a rod you'll also face choices for handle styles. Grip

shapes include: reverse half wells, cigar, half wells and full wells. The reverse half wells, where the cork is thick at the butt, tapers down slightly, then swells where your palm meets the cork, and again tapers down as it meets the rod blank, is the most popular style on modern freshwater fly rods. This is the shape you'll see on about 99 percent of the rods sold today. Most grips are made of cork, or rings of cork glued together and cut to a specific profile. Cork provides a sure grip and comfortable surface for your hand even when wet. Cork's use as a grip could be short lived, however. Wineries are already replacing cork with plastic or other synthetic materials because of a reported shortage of cork. As cork prices rise, anglers might also see other grip materials finding their way onto fly rods. The future could be very interesting and I'm certain the materials will be as varied as the materials used to build fly rods over the centuries.

Some insiders reveal that the way the rod feels in your hand is the best guess on how you and the rod will work as a team. The perfect rod is nothing more than an extension of your body and arm. Almost every grip feels a little different so you have to be the judge about what feels good in your hand.

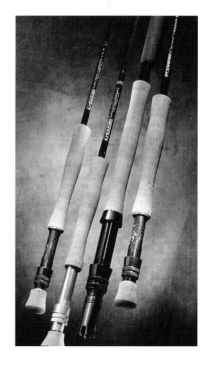

Most fly rod grips, such as the ones shown below, are made of cork, harvested from the bark of the European cork oak tree. Cork's elasticity near-impermeability makes it an ideal material for fishing rod grips.

Look for Detail and Fine Finish

When selecting a rod, take a close look at the rod and inspect its handle, eyes and tip for excess or bulging glue beads, frayed threads, or other abnormalities. Look for attention to detail in the finishing of brass or metal reel attachment hardware, hardwood reel seats and the rod's overall finish. I recommend avoiding rods with plastic reel locks since these can easily become cross-threaded thanks to sand and dirt, a situation that can cause a lot of frustration. The same rule applies for plastic reel seats and other cost-cutting parts found on some mass-produced rods. You'll save money and frustration by buying a rod with metal components.

BUILDING A BAMBOO PUZZLE

Bamboo rods are generally built up from hundreds of slivers of bamboo that have been precision planed to fit together at specific angles and in specified lengths. The bamboo is precut, then placed in a jig and planed to a required dimension. The sections of cane are then glued together, and the rod is finished in steps similar to building a standard rod. The handwork required to plane and assemble the pieces makes bamboo rods expensive. Some rod builders have been issued patents on their angle and design concepts for building these types of rods.

Some rod manufacturers have begun to use double-foot snake guides—these look like a single piece of curly twisted wire—to cut down on the rod's weight. If the rod you're considering has a single foot guide—a ring protruding above a single point of attachment—inspect the inside of the ring and look for details such as the finish or a ceramic or other material inserted inside the ring. Most stripping guides—the big eye nearest the rod's grip—are single foot and here's a place to inspect closely for quality. The smoother and more finished the inner surface of the guide is, the easier the rod should cast line.

Next, of what material is the rod blank made? Fiberglass is out these days, and graphite and other space-age materials—such as thermoplastic enriched resins—are in. Boron and carbon are two other rod production materials. Bamboo also has a strong following but finely crafted bamboo rods can cost thousands of dollars and are not the ideal starter rod. Save that purchase for when you're rich and famous or wanting to become a purist fly fisherman.

Today's angler is in the best position when selecting a rod than any generation of anglers has ever been. There are many superb companies that are producing real fly rod works of art (see Appendix). Purchasing an expensive rod can bring satisfaction of ownership, can increase your success rate in some instances by increasing feel and response, and can motivate you to fish more often because of your financial investment. I enjoy looking at and holding expensive rods even when I'm not buying a new rod.

The good news is that many of the starter rods available to fly anglers today are better than the best-of-the-best of a decade ago. Some manufacturers relieve the buyer of some of the guesswork and offer packages that include the rod, a matching reel, the backing and fly line, and a fly. Many makers include a tube and sock to protect your rod and a zippered case to protect your reel. You'll need these if you fish often. Some manufacturers go a step further and include a video and booklet to show you how to get started, how to select and buy a rod, and how to rig it up and begin fishing. Some of these packages are a very good buy for the money, and a few are not.

The Price Factor

An important factor to consider when selecting a rod is cost. I evaluate the cost of a rod based on how much I will use it over a season or two, then divide the hours into the dollars to get a good idea of the rod's cost effectiveness. You can find fly rods that cost less than $100 and some that cost more than $700. A good rule of thumb is to buy the best that you can afford. The more you enjoy the performance of a rod,

the more you will be enticed to take it fishing, and the more cost effective it becomes over time.

Is there a difference between good rods and great rods? Yes. My wife, Reuth, went with me one weekend to a rod manufacturer's demonstration at our local fly shop. After the presentation, attendees could select and cast with any rod that they wished. Reuth displayed an almost shocked look when she switched from casting the company's cheapest rod—around $200—to casting the most expensive, top-of-the-line model that cost more than $700. She did not buy a rod that day, but she was well on her way to discovering the quality of performance that a top rod has to offer. The next time that we went fishing, she asked to try the upper-end rod I was casting. She was so impressed by the sensitive feel, responsiveness, balance and many other performance factors—including the finish—that she too decided that $600 was a worthwhile investment in happiness if you like to fish. I agree with her.

Will one rod do it all? No. If you fly-fish a great deal, you'll quickly discover that you probably have more rods than you need, but never as many as you want. For me, owning a dozen rods has worked out well. I use almost all of them every year while traveling to faraway angling destinations or while wading into my local streams. Some I've built, and others are top-of-the-line rods from premium manufacturers,

TIP:

Priceless Personalization
To add a personal touch to your fly rod, try having the butt cap (the dime-sized metal cap located on the end of most fly rods) engraved with your initials. Many jewelry stores and trophy engraving shops can perform this service for less than $20. This is a great way to identify your rod in case of theft. Some fly shops also employ skilled artists who will write your name on your fly rod for a nominal fee. They use a gold liquid ink to permanently inscribe your name on the rod shaft in front of the handle.

FLY RODS: BUILD YOUR OWN

Looking for a great way to learn more about fly-fishing and to save money so you have more funds to spend on fishing trips? Consider building your own rods. With minimal skills and tools, plus a few materials and some epoxy, you can build a quality rod in a few hours. The most important part of the process is patience and not rushing to make mistakes. Once you learn the basics with your first completed rod, the rest will come easier and quicker. The best part is building a rod unlike any other found on the market —custom built to meet your needs and wishes. Here are the basic steps to begin the process:

Step 1

Order the components, including cork handle, blank, eyes, thread, hook keeper, winding check, tip, epoxy and reel seat. You will also need a set of stands and a round cork file. A spool holder or rod wrapper is also handy to tension the thread to create more uniform wraps. You can also place the spool of thread in a cup and run the thread through a phone book to create tension.

You can order a complete rod kit from most major rod manufacturers and retailers. Kits are good for beginners because they remove much of the frustration of guessing which eyes to use. Your local fly shop should be able to help you find the best combination of materials and the equipment that you'll need.

Step 2

You'll need to find the spine of the rod—the stiffest side—and mark it. Roll the blank with the large end on a tabletop while holding the smaller end in your hand. Bend the blank at a 45 degree angle and roll it back and forth. You'll feel the blank stiffen on one side—that's the spine. Mark the spine of all sections in marker on a wrap of masking tape. Your rod's eyes will be attached to the spine.

Step 3

Measure the blanks and determine where the eyes will be located. These again are best indicated with a ½-inch wrap of masking tape that can be easily removed as you build the rod.

Step 4

Prepare the grip with a cork reamer so that it slides into place against the reel seat. To fit the reel seat, lightly sand the blank and wrap layers of masking tape until the seat and butt fit tightly. Coat blank and masking tape with two-part epoxy and quickly assemble all parts, including the cork grip. Snug the parts together, aligned with the rod's spine. Place the cap on the end of the reel seat and then permit the components to dry in place.

Step 8
Wrap the female ends of the ferrule, and attach the hook keeper just in front of the handle.

Add any butt wrap, decals or other ornament. Miniature trout decals add a nice touch here.

Step 5
Use a piece of ½-inch masking tape to secure the largest guide in place on the rod blank on the spine side. Put the blank on the stands and begin wrapping the thread about ¼ inch behind the tip of the eye's foot. Wrap the thread upon itself for 4 to 5 wraps. Keep the wraps uniform and tight to the eye's foot and then up onto the eye. Cut off any excess from the lead end of the thread. Remove the masking tape. When you get to within 4 or 5 wraps of where you plan to stop—where the eye turns up sharply—put a small loop of thread under the thread on the opposite side of the blank, away from the eye. When you complete the last wrap, grasp the rod eye and thread between two fingers. Cut the thread with about 2 inches of extra length and pass this through the loop you secured under the wraps. Tug the loop ends firmly and evenly to pull the ends of the thread underneath the wraps and out. Carefully trim off any excess. Always work from the blank and up onto the eye's foot as you wrap.

Repeat this process for each eye and keep them in line with the spine.

Step 6
Secure the tip on the smallest end of the blank with hot glue. This is so you can replace the tip if the rod is broken, and that is the point where most breaks occur.

Step 7
Put the rod together and visually check it for alignment. Re-inspect each wrap and carefully remove any protruding thread ends.

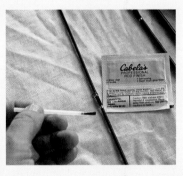

Step 9
After a final check of eye alignment—this is important to help your fly line smoothly pass along the rod—begin brushing on the rod finish. Again, take your time and do a professional job as you cover all threads. Next, place the rod on the stands and turn it a ½-turn every 15 minutes to keep the finish from running to one side and creating a bump. You can add a second coat of finish if you need to and again turn the rod until the finish is dry. Depending upon humidity and the finish type, this process could take up to 2 hours.

Step 10
Go fishing and try your new rod.

TIP:

Try a Rod Tube
Leave your fly rod unrigged and stored in its rod tube or sock to greatly reduce the chances of rod damage or breakage, and you'll spend less time fighting brush. Store the rob tube concealed in brush when you start fishing. Pick it up and repack your rod on your return trip.

while a few are specialty rods acquired for specific situations—such as when the steelheads run in the Great Lakes region.

How Many Parts?

In recent years more anglers have begun to travel to top destinations or for the pleasure of seeing new water and the scenic countryside where trout live. Manufacturers have made travel with a fly rod easier by breaking away from the standard lengthy 2-piece rod to produce 4-, 5- and sometimes 7-piece fly rods. These rods can sometimes be more expensive, but will be

worth the money if you travel often. The standard 4-piece travel rod in its tube is approximately 30 inches long. You can slip most travel rods into your hard-side luggage to prevent theft or breakage. The standard 2-piece rod in a tube is approximately 58 inches long. This will not fit in a suitcase.

I would never recommend checking a 2-piece rod in a standard fly rod tube as luggage with any airline. You might never see your rod again. Consider buying a sturdy, lockable rod vault if you will be traveling. You might find that your rod, or numerous rods, while safely packed in rod tubes, will also fit inside a lockable gun case. The extra padding, sturdy frames and corners, and lockable option will help increase the chances that you and your rods arrive at your destination together. Some airlines will still let you carry a 2-piece rod onto the airplane and other airlines refuse to accommodate any fly rod. If in doubt, call ahead and ask. Then call again and recheck since airlines have been known to give conflicting information to travelers. Yes, this happened to me.

On-Site Assembly Required

What should you do with a rod when you have arrived at your destination and are ready to start casting or fishing? First, insert the

CARE AS YOU TRAVEL

One last note about rods. Always use a soft sock to cover your rod and a durable tube to store your rod in. Once you arrive at your fishing destination, get the gear tossing, door slamming and other shuffling completed before you settle down and uncase your rod. As soon as you return to the vehicle, cabin or destination, the fly rod should be the first thing stored in its case. Do not lean a rod against a car or near a car door unless you want to buy a new fly rod. This is where most rod breaking accidents occur. And when you're home or in a room at the lodge, open the case and let your rod dry. This is a good time to check for cracks and damage as you wipe away any dirt or smudges on the rod's finish with a soft cloth. Many times when a rod fails it's the result of seasons of abuse and neglect.

correct tapered pieces (male) into the matching ferrule openings (female) with the guides offset at 90 degrees. Next, gently twist the sections until the guides are aligned. Some rods have dots that connect when the rod is correctly assembled. You can create this system on any rod with a light touch of colored fingernail polish. It is worth noting that with some rods, such as the Orvis Trident TLS, the two sections will not completely meet to close the gap at the ferrules. This is designed to increase the life of the rod and keep the ferrules from becoming worn and easily separated. When in doubt about

the fit, never force two sections together. Ask a fly shop or contact the rod's manufacturer.

Before you pull fly line through the stripping guide—the large guide closest to the handle—turn the rod over, point it skyward and visually sight along the rod to be certain that all the guides are aligned and in a descending order of size from rear to the tip. With the new 7-piece rods, assembly takes some time. One of the benefits of the 2- or 4-piece rods is that you can get your rig assembled quicker and be on the water and fishing faster.

TIP:

Borrow or Rent?
The best option is to rent a fly rod. Many shops have rental and demo models. Some shops rent high-end models hoping that you'll fall in love with the rig.
I've tried very expensive rod and reel combos on trips through rentals that I will probably never be able to afford.

SHOPPING FOR A FLY ROD

You can often contact a fly rod manufacturer to determine the types of fly rods that they produce and sell, plus gather information about which rod they might recommend. Some companies also provide prices while others can guide you to local dealers. Some companies will send you a free catalog and others have Web sites with all of the information posted. Here are some great places to search for fly rods:

Cabela's
One Cabela Drive
Sidney, NE 69160
(800) 237-4444
www.cabelas.com

G. Loomis
1359 Down River Rd.
Woodland, WA 98674
(800) 662-8818
www.gloomis.com

Martin Classic Fly Tackle
PO Box 270
Tulsa, OK 74101
(918) 836-5581
www.martinfishing.com

Powell and Co.
11300-E Trade Center Drive
Rancho Cordova, CA 95742
(888) 635-9763
www.powellco.com

Redington
820 SE Dixie Highway
Stuart, FL 34994-3803
(800) 253-2538
www.redington.com

R.L. Winston Rod Co.
500 S. Main Street
Twin Bridges, MT 59754
(406) 684-5674
www.winstonrods.com

Sage
8500 NE Day Road
Bainbridge Island, WA 98110
(800) 533-3004
www.sageflyfish.com

Scientific Anglers
3M Center, Building 223-4NE-05
St. Paul, MN 55144
(800) 525-6290
www.scientificanglers.com

Scott Fly Rod Company
2355 Air Park Way
Montrose, CO 81401
(800) 728-7208
www.scottflyrod.com

St. Croix
PO Box 279
Park Falls, WI 54552
(800) 826-7042
www.stcroixrods.com

The Orvis Company
Rt 7
Manchester, VT 05254
(888) 235-9763
www.orvis.com

Reels from various manufacturers offer different handles, feels, line capacities, operation and other features. Make your choice based on your rod and how much you are willing to spend.

3 | The Reel Thing

**BLACK NOSE
DACE**

(Streamer)
Popular Sizes:
06, 08, 10
Hook Type:
4X long streamer
Thread:
Black 6/0
Tail:
*Short stubby red wool if
using flat silver tinsel for
body.*
Body:
*Flat silver tinsel or fine
silver Mylar piping.*
Ribbing:
*Oval silver tinsel if body
is flat silver tinsel.*
Wing:
*Brown bucktail over
black dyed squirrel tail or
bucktail over sparse white
bucktail.*
Tag:
*red 3/0 thread to secure end
of Mylar piping body.*

The time when you are in a fly shop perusing the fly rod selection is also a great time to handle and select a matching reel. You'll face a daunting task since there are seemingly unlimited numbers of reels to choose from with more models being released each year. In one flyfishing equipment catalog alone I counted more than 300 reel models and variations, with prices ranging from $39 to $1,500. You can find reels that cost as much as $5,000. Wow, are fly anglers and trout enthusiasts lucky these days or simply overwhelmed? I believe the answer is a mix of both.

The primary purpose of a reel is to help you manage line, including storage and release. Extra tasks for the reel include helping you winch in fish, smoothly release more line for longer casts and get more performance from your rod. A reputable editor at a national fishing magazine once told me that he bought inexpensive reels because they were simply places to store fly line. Shortly after making those comments he recounted a story about how one of his reels had "exploded" while he was trying to winch in a steelhead in the Great Lakes area. The fish escaped and

his big fishing adventure was cut short because his reel had failed. Lesson learned.

Selecting a Reel

Most reels are designed with an outer housing shell and an independent inner spool. The reel housing can be cast, machined or molded from a graphite or plastic-like material. While most reels are a dull black color to reduce or prevent fish spooking glare, some reels are silver or gold. The spools inside a reel can be metal or plastic, and may be produced as solid pieces or with multiple small holes to help water escape. Some reels offered today give anglers the option of buying additional spools so that you can easily change lines according to the fishing conditions. This is a great option to consider.

You'll find three basic reel types at most fly shops and sporting goods stores—single-action, multiplying and automatic. Single-action reels are popular lightweight units that are easy to operate and maintain. One turn of the handle results in one complete turn of the spool.

This Orvis Battenkill reel is one of America's most popular models. It is matched to the rod for a balanced feel and smooth casting.

PARTS OF A REEL

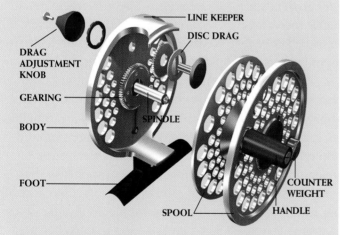

- DRAG ADJUSTMENT KNOB
- LINE KEEPER
- DISC DRAG
- GEARING
- BODY
- SPINDLE
- FOOT
- COUNTER WEIGHT
- SPOOL
- HANDLE

THE MATERIALS

Reels today are constructed of many materials. I've encountered models made of plastic, nylon, graphite, die cast and machined aluminum, stainless steel and titanium. Some reels are painted, others are anodized and some models are coated with proprietary durable finishes. While flashy brass reels might look impressive to you, there could be concerns that a flash of reflected sunlight might spook a wary trout. You be the judge.

Multiplying reels are designed so that a complete revolution of the handle around the circumference of the reel results in one-and-a-half or more revolutions of the inner spool. This is handy when fishing where long line retrieves are common. Large arbor multiplying reels are gaining a growing legion of followers each year.

Automatic reels, once the rave, are powered by a coil spring. The spring is tightened when fly line is pulled out, by pressing a lever that protrudes in front of the reel near the rod's grip; the spring is released and unwinds to tug the line back onto the spool. In addition to spring failure, however, ever present fine grit and messy sand seems to attack these reels and cause failures and line jams. Few automatic reels are used or produced today.

You'll face other choices when selecting a reel, including the selection of a drag system. Reel drag will help to keep your line from tangling when you strip out line by keeping the inner spool from freewheeling. Drag also helps tire a running trout by exerting tension on the spool and line. A uniform and properly adjusted drag can help prevent breakage of tippets and help you land fish. On some reels you'll notice a small weight opposite the handle to help keep the spool counterbalanced when you're cranking in line during the heat of the action.

Two common types of drag are the ratchet-and-pawl and disk drag. The ratchet-and-pawl uses a gear system and makes an audible clicking noise when engaged. This is the most popular system and most ratchet-and-pawl models have a wide range of adjustment options. Adjusting the reel drag properly can help prevent a fish from breaking your leader or tippet.

Disk drag reels normally have a layer of cork or synthetic material that applies pressure to the side of the spool. These materials can wear out if you fish often or do not remove sand and grit on a frequent

basis. Disk-type reels, however, are quiet to operate. Some have exposed spools so that you can apply pressure directly to the edge of the reel when you're struggling with a fish. This can be a valuable option to prevent break-offs if you're fishing some of the larger rivers or from a drift boat.

The Capacity Question

Other elements to take into consideration when buying a reel are line capacity, whether the reel will be left- or right-handed or reversible and how much money you wish to pull from your wallet. To help you determine a reel's line capacity, most manufacturers print the details in their brochures or on the box so you can easily discover the facts. If you see WF5F/100, this translates into a capacity for a standard weight-forward 5-weight floating fly line with 100 yards of backing. If you cannot determine the facts, ask a representative at the fly shop or call the manufacturer.

Many reels on the market today will permit the user to easily switch from a left- or right-handed configuration. If you have questions, ask the dealer.

Another good consideration when buying a reel is to ask the fly shop or store to load the spool with backing and fly line. Most shops

BLUE WINGED OLIVE

(Dry Fly)
Popular Sizes:
14, 16, 18, 20, 22
Hook Type:
Extra-fine dry fly
Thread:
Olive—6/0 or 8/0
Tail:
Dark dun hackle fibers
Body:
Medium olive fur
Wing:
Dark dun hackle tips
Hackle:
Dark dun

FLY REELS

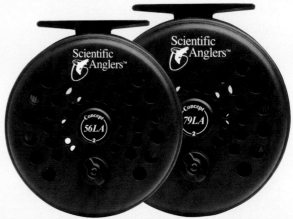

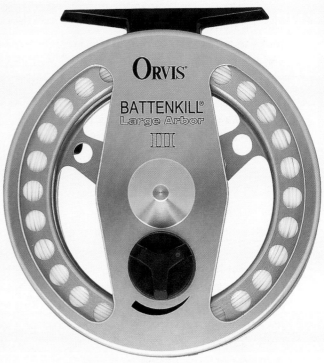

Fly reels, such as these Orvis models, use either click-and-pawl or disk drags. Disk drags are more effective when fishing for really large fish while traditional click-and-pawl type drags, used with fine tippets, are usually more effective for most trout species.

have machines that can easily and quickly accomplish this chore, and many fly shops will perform this task for free. You'll want to hold on to the empty line spool and all printed materials that came with the reel and fly line for future reference and for storage purposes if you change the fly line in the future. You can easily load backing and fly line into a reel at home if you wish but the task requires a little patience and knowledge of knots.

rinse away sand and remove any gummy gear grease. A toothpick can be helpful for this chore. Once the reel is cleaned, the next stage of the task involves carefully re-greasing and re-oiling gears, springs and other parts. If you have a disk drag avoid getting oil and grease on the cork or resistant surface. You should also

Reel Care

It is a fact of life that flowing water erodes rocks and makes sand. It is also a fact of life that sand will find its way into your reel's inner workings. Routine reel maintenance can help you receive a lifetime of dependable service from most well-constructed reels. After studying the manufacturer's guidelines, you can remove the spool and then

TUBE-STYLE ROD AND REEL CASES

COMBINATION TUBE CASE
AND KIT BAG

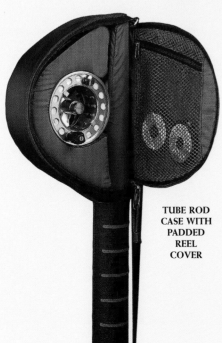

TUBE ROD
CASE WITH
PADDED
REEL
COVER

A STRONG CASE FOR CASES

Imagine the horror that everyone in the car experienced when we heard something slide across the roof of the car and turned to see a fly reel land on the pavement and tumble into the ditch. Our horror was short lived when we determined that the case had protected the reel from dents and scratches. Whether you choose a case of leather, neoprene, nylon or some other material, you should always store your reel in a case while traveling. Always!

When you return home or to the cabin at the end of the day, be sure to remove the reel and permit it and the case to dry thoroughly before long-term storage. This will prevent damaging rust. It's not a bad idea to clean it as well.

avoid getting oil and grease on the fly line since petroleum products can erode the line's surface. If you need reel repairs, some manufacturers have repair shops. There are also specialty shops that repair reels. Check the yellow pages or Internet to find a shop near you.

Another way to increase the life of your reel is to store it in a reel case. Bumps and contact with hard surfaces can become nicks and burrs on metal surfaces, or worse, result in a damaged reel frame. There are many good fleece-lined cases and neoprene covers on the market to wrap around and protect your reels when they are not in use. If you use a fleece- or simulated sheepskin-lined case, be certain that the reel and case are dry before you store them or the lining may trap moisture and cause rust and ultimately reel failure.

A Question of Cost

How much should you spend on a reel? A good rule is about one-fourth to one-half of the price of the rod that it will be combined with. Your local fly shop or any reputable flyfishing outfitter can provide a selection of reels to help find the one that perfectly matches your fly rod. In some cases manufacturers sell rod and reel kits preassembled to save you the guesswork.

Reels are more than places to store line. A good reel works like a sturdy winch, helps you land trout and looks like a piece of art at the end of a long day on the river. Take care of it and you'll enjoy years of use.

SHOPPING FOR A REEL BARGAIN?

Here are some reel manufacturers that you can contact to obtain information about the models and price ranges that they offer.

Cabela's
(800) 237-4444
www.cabelas.com

Cortland
(607) 756-2851

Eagle Claw
(303) 321-1481

Fly Logic
(208) 495-2090

Fly Tech
(800) 590-2281

G. Loomis
(800) 662-8818
www.gloomis.com

Loop
(800) 322-3218

Orvis
(888) 235-9763
www.orvis.com

Pflueger
(803) 754-7000

Redington
(800) 253-2538
www.redington.com

Sage
(800) 533-3004
www.sageflyfish.com

Scientific Anglers
(800) 525-6290
www.scientific
anglers.com

Fly lines are designed to shoot smoothly through a rod's eyes.
Recent developments in line technology have created lines that cast
farther with less surface resistance.

4 | The Fine Fly Line

While fly rods and reels are important to anglers, the fly line and its extensions—the backing, leader and tippet—are the connection between you and a trout. Make the right choice and the fish will be in your hand or net. Choose poorly and you'll be left only with a fish tale.

Fly lines perform the important task of carrying your lure—the fly—through the air and gently placing it in the water at the precise point that you select. Standard rod and reel anglers use the weight of the lure—such as a heavy treble-hooked balsa wood bass plug—to drag the monofilament along behind. Instead of the dog wagging the tail, when using a fly line you're asking the tail to wag the dog. The fly line system works and I've seen professional casters gently place a fly in a shoe across the length of a basketball court. Some casters can cast with such finesse that the dainty dry fly under their command drifts onto the water's surface with much less disturbance than real insects cast naturally by Mother Nature.

The Options

Fly lines come in many weights, colors, styles, tapers and buoyancies. Some are designed to float, while others are designed to sink at variable rates. Most lines are constructed around a core of fine strands coated with an air-filled polymer shell. Sinking lines replace the air bubbles with small particles of lead, tungsten or other heavy material. Like rods and reels, prices can vary from $20 to more than $100 for each line.

Your most important decision is in choosing a line that matches your rod's weight and your reel's capacity and weight classification. You'll find these critical numbers printed in the manufacturer's brochure, on reel shipping boxes or the side of the fly rod shaft. The ultimate goal is choosing components that will feel balanced in your hand, cast like a fine automobile drives and that work to help you land a trout. With hundreds of options available, you should be able to find a fly line that meets your needs.

BRASSIE

(Nymph)
Popular Sizes:
14, 16, 18, 20
Hook Type:
2X long nymph
Thread:
Black 8/0
Abdomen:
Fine copper wire
Thorax:
Peacock herl

Fly line is your vital link between you and the trout. Select the right line for the job and to match your rod and reel.

You'll find the line's weight printed on the box. Line lengths range from 80 to 100 feet, but the first 30 feet is normally the section measured and judged to meet the standard set by the American Sportfishing Association. Fly lines can range from 1- to 12-weight with 1-weight being very light and 12-weight being very heavy and difficult for most anglers to cast. Most anglers use 4- to 7-weight lines for most fishing situations. The weight of a line is determined by weighing the first 30 feet of the line in grains. The standard classification of a fly line is printed on the packaging as a number, for example 5-wt., 6-wt. for 5- and 6-weight lines.

The weight of a line helps determine its finesse or the ability to shoulder its way through wind. Lightweight lines in the 1-through 4-weight category help cast tiny flies for short distances. There is simply not enough weight in the line to move the

mass over great distances no matter how much leverage and force you impart. On the upside, these lines are great for casting nearly microscopic flies, like the Tricos. Small lightweight lines can help you catch ultra-spooky trout where heavier weight lines would cause too much water disturbance and make the fish head for cover. Some anglers fish light, thinner lines later in the summer when trout waters tend to be lower and clearer.

Next in line are the medium-weight fly lines, sizes 4 through 7 that cast well in most situations and will handle a wide variety of fly sizes. It takes a sturdy and stiff line to propel a heavier weight fly. Medium-weight lines offer anglers the most versatility when casting flies across a wide spectrum of American waters.

At the upper end of the scale are the 8-weights and above. These big boys will move large lures through stiff winds with ease. However, you give up some finesse and heavy lines will spook trout under some conditions. On the other hand, these big lines will pass through walls of wind and carry really big flies.

Swim or Sink?

While a fly line's taper—or lack thereof—can strongly influence its castability, the question arises

of what do you want the line to do once it lands on the water's surface. Do you want the fly line to sink along with the weighted nymph ahead of it or do you want the line to ride high and dry on the surface with a coated dry fly? Simply stated do you want the line to float or sink?

Floating lines are designed to ride on the water's surface and not sink pulling your fly down. Floating lines cast well and newly developed coatings—such as Orvis' Wonderline—have made them much slicker so anglers can cast farther. If you switch to a nymph and want it to sink, simply add weight, such as a split shot, to the tippet

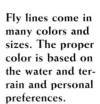

Fly lines come in many colors and sizes. The proper color is based on the water and terrain and personal preferences.

These packaged tapered leaders require only two knots—one to attach to the fly line and one to secure the fly at the thinnest end. When the thin forward section of the leader is shortened after tying on several flies, you can tie on tippet material to extend the life of the leader.

Which Color of Fly Line?

above the fly. In a deep pool, however, floating line could prevent your fly from reaching the the depth where the trout are. If this happens, then you'll need to switch to a sinking line or add more weight above the fly.

Sinking lines contain small bits of lead or tungsten to make them sink. Obviously the more lead and tungsten in the coating, the heavier the line is and the faster it dives. Some manufacturers provide sink rates to tell of how fast the line dives. Sometimes you'll need to place the fly deep and fast, other times you might need a fly to meander its way down.

On the downside, sinking lines go underwater and can be difficult to retrieve and cast. You almost have to reel some lines completely in before you can cast again and this can eat up precious fishing time. Under most situations you can place the fly deep by using weighted bodies and larger split shot.

Fly line colors can vary from yellow-green to orange to tan. Your color selection should be based on that which is easiest for you to see on the water. Some anglers argue around campfires about what color of fly line is likely to spook trout. They base their arguments on the color of the vegetation growing along the banks of a stream or lake. If you have doubts or concerns, buy several colors in the same style, such as a 5-weight WF (weight forward) line, and test them yourself. You can easily do this by buying additional reel spools that are easily changed. Then all you have to do is fish often and keep a detailed log. Need any other reasons to go fishing more often?

Another consideration in fly lines is the taper. Most lines are not uniform in diameter along their length. Some lines taper at the front section and some lines—such as the double taper—are reduced in diameter at each end. Double-tapered lines are normally 4-weight or less. These lines have a short plump section to help move the fly as you cast and a nimble thinner front portion that gently delivers the fly to the water's surface. With a double-tapered line you can increase the line's life by unspooling it and switching ends. The fly line box will indicate double taper with DT.

Weight forward lines rule today's trout rivers and are the most common type purchased by fly fishers. These lines are designed with most of the weight contained in the line's first 30-foot span. They are good beginning standards and cast well in winds. WF indicates that the line is weight forward.

Two other line configurations are available. Shooting tapers have a short thick section attached to monofilament or coated Dacron. While some anglers can cast a shooting taper head up to 100 feet, they sacrifice precise control and the excess line length can be difficult to manage. On the other end of the line spectrum is level line which has no taper or bulk anywhere along its span. This line can be difficult to cast and manage.

In Back

Fly line is never loaded directly onto a reel. A more durable and smaller-diameter material—back-

KEEPING TRACK

Most fly line manufacturers include a stick-on decal with the line that you can place on your reel to remind you what type of line is wound on the reel. I highly recommend using these since you will have trouble remembering what line is on what reel as you accumulate more fishing gear. Another helpful idea is to keep the manufacturer's box and shipping spool. You can use it to store your fly line if you need to have a reel repaired or if you remove the line for some other reason.

Remember the information about the manufacturer's weight classification of a rod printed in the rod's blank just forward of the handle? This number helps you select the right weight line for that rod. My personal experience—and it's confirmed by other anglers—is that you can move a number above or below the specified rod number and not make great sacrifices in rod performance. Some rods are actually classified as a 5/6-weight or similar number. I wouldn't make it a point to fish 5-weight line in a 4-weight rod all the time, but if you're casting into a blustery early spring wind and need more control, moving up in weight might be the ticket for a great day on the water. Later, as summer weather and conditions ensue, you might move down and fish a 3-weight line in a 4-weight rod to daintily deliver a small fly to spooky trout. Remember that most fly line weight numbers are merely guidelines.

down side, you have to carry many spools of line and those spools can take up valuable space in a fishing vest or pack. The knots that join sections of leader material are more easily caught on underwater obstructions and fouled by algae. If you like to do everything for yourself, however, this might be the route for you.

ing—is placed on the reel first. Tie backing to the center of the spool with a Duncan knot. Make sure the knot is firm and seated on the center of the spool. The back of the fly line is then tied to the backing and the line is cranked onto the reel spool. Most manufacturers provide information about a reel's line and backing capacity.

On the other side are one-piece leaders that taper from the butt (the thick rear section that's tied to the fly line) to the tip. Improved manufacturing processes in recent years have made these leaders stronger, more uniform and more affordable. Many arrive with three or four leaders per pack and the small packages are easily stored in a vest pocket. Most leaders are available in 9- and 12-foot lengths.

The Leader Goes First

On the forward end of the fly line is tied a leader, and then a tippet to which the fly is attached. Leaders normally range from 9 to 12 feet long. Some anglers like to tie together sections of monofilament to create their own leaders. There are numerous formulas for creating leaders but, on the

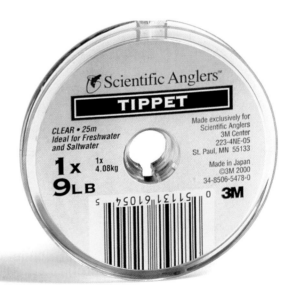

Both the one-piece and constructed leaders will get shorter with use as you tie on and remove a fly. This loss of the thinner end of the leader shifts the fly closer to thicker material which can be more easily noticed by trout. After the first 6 to 10 inches of a leader are removed, you can tie on fine tippet material to extend the life of your leader and cause less trout spooking water disturbance. A Blood Knot or Triple Surgeon's Knot works well for this task. The thickness of the tippet material will depend upon what fly you are tying on, the clarity of the water and the size of fish in the water where you'll be casting. The larger the number, such as an 8X or 7X material, the smaller in diameter the tippet is and the more easily it will break. Experimentation is often the best way to determine what materials and methods work best for your style of fishing and casting.

LINE MAINTENANCE AND CARE

When does a fly line need replacing? Much of this depends on where you fish, how often and how you care for your line. If the fly line's coating becomes cracked or rough to the touch, then it's time to buy a new fly line—period. When a line becomes stiff and brittle, it is harder to manipulate and cast so your fishing enjoyment will decline. Err on the safe side and replace a fly line when you have doubts or see any changes in the line's performance. Since the fly line is the only link between you and a trout, you need to be certain the line will perform when the time comes.

Many manufacturers recommend gently washing a fly line after use with a sponge or soft cloth in warm soapy water. Cleaning helps remove abrasive sand and algae or other matter from the fly line. Allow the line to dry thoroughly before you wind it back onto the reel and store it. This is also a great time to inspect the fly line for possible cuts that can reduce the line's strength.

A few fly lines come with line dressing and a small sponge. Always follow the manufacturer's recommendations. I would not recommend dressing a line unless the manufacturer recommends it because some solutions can damage the new generation of line finishes.

If you are not going to use your fly rod, reel and line for an extended period of time, you should remove the line and store it in large loose coils on a line holder in a cool dry place. This could help extend the line's life. Remember to tag the line so that you know the weight and taper. You might also want to keep a log that indicates when the line was purchased and how many hours you use it each month or season.

Never store a reel with wet fly line in a reel case. Moisture can cause mold and deterioration of the line's coating. Bright sunlight, the source of ultraviolet (UV) radiation, is worse than moisture at attacking a fly line's coating. Never leave your rod and reel in direct sunlight for any period of time.

If you have questions or concerns about a fly line, contact the line manufacturer. Most provide toll-free numbers or Web site addresses on the printed material that is shipped along with the line.

*Proper grip will help you control the rod and
keep your hand from tiring too quickly.*

5 | *Cast Away*

CDC ELK WING CADDIS

(Dry Fly)
Popular Sizes:
12, 14, 16, 18, 20
Additional Colors:
Tan, gray, olive, or peacock
Hook Type:
Extra-fine dry fly
Thread:
6/0 tan
Body:
Dubbing or peacock herl
Ribbing:
Fine flat gold tinsel
Wing:
Underwing: gray CDC fibers.
Overwing: bleached elk hair.
Other Materials:
Antennae: pair or stripped brown hackle stems almost as long as the body.

Casting is the motion of the rod created and coordinated by your arms and hands to propel the line, and the fly attached to the end of it, to your intended target on the water.

If there is one major source of frustration for most anglers, it's casting.

Numerous books, in numbers capable of filling large libraries have been written about casting. There have even been multiple videos released on the subject in recent years. All of these are great sources to pick up pointers, but casting can only be learned and perfected in one way—by practice. The more you practice, the better at casting you will become. In fact, casting is much like riding a bicycle—once you master it, it's simple.

The idea of a correct casting style and correct casting method are myths at best. Since no two humans are built exactly alike or have arms, wrists and hands that are the same, no two humans will cast exactly alike. Physical skill and coordination are also factors. After experiment and a basic introduction, each angler that I've met seems to have developed their own style that works best for

them. You will find that you too will develop your own "style" once you learn the basics.

If you want to cast farther or learn to place a fly in difficult spots, such as under the brush of overhanging tree limbs, consider enrolling in a casting school. There are many schools held across the nation each spring and summer. During the winter months, many fly shops host free or low-cost casting clinics. Many guides can also give personalized instruction and helpful pointers. No need to be embarrassed to ask about or try to learn more about casting. I like to attend classes and clinics each year to learn new techniques and refresh the details that I already know.

The Movement

Each cast has two parts: the back cast when the rod's forward section, tip and fly line pass behind your shoulder and head, and the forward cast when the rod tip and fly line are ahead of your position. The law of physics holds very true in casting: for every action, there is an equal and opposite reaction. The

Backyard practice sessions can be helpful to increase distance and precision casting.

rhythm, along with clean abrupt stops, are far more important for executing a good cast than brute force. Once you master the rhythm, you can make rapid gains in your casting length and precision placement.

One of the most common mistakes for most anglers is rushing a cast. If you hear the fly line and leader crack behind you, you are moving too fast. This crack is the line hitting itself or the leader. When you cast properly, you should feel the rod's forward length and tip jerk backward on a back cast. Look over your shoulder and watch your back cast to see this motion. The jerk and tug that you feel in your hand is the rod loading up under the weight and force of the line.

Prepare a Perfect Practice Session

back cast is important and sets the stage for what happens during the forward cast. If you are having problems with your cast or decide to experiment with new or different casting techniques, watch your back cast.

Casting is a plane affair. The tip of your rod should move smoothly along a plane or imaginary straight line as if your rod were a long paintbrush and you were painting an overhead ceiling without lowering the brush. Proper timing and

A properly prepared practice area will help you gain insight into your cast rapidly. Water grips the fly line while you are fishing, and if you can practice casting on a lake or body of water, you'll learn more. If you can't practice on water, the grass in a lawn works well. Avoid paved or gravel parking lots since these rough surfaces will abrade and destroy your fly line.

Most casts range in distance from 20 to 50 feet. You'll want about 60 feet of unobstructed space in front of and behind you when practicing. The area should be clear of overhead telephone and power lines and other obstructions such as tree limbs.

When you rig up your fly rod and reel, always tie a leader to the fly line. To help you visually follow the line and leader, attach a small piece of brightly colored yarn to the end of the leader to imitate your fly.

Placing multiple targets—a Frisbee or plate works best—around your location will help you practice for precision placement. Any training aid should be easily moved and should not have sharp edges to cut your line or protruding prongs

and places that could cause your line to tangle. It's important to keep frustration opportunities to a minimum so you can concentrate on rhythm and form.

The Basics

In flyfishing and casting, the fly line does the work to carry your fly the distance from you to the water and out to the trout. The rod moves the fly line, and your arm—especially the forearm— moves the fly rod. It's important to note that:

▶ The fly line and your fly go where the rod's tip points as you cast.

Tight casting quarters and short distances can be mastered with on-stream practice and experience.

arm movement are important to help the rod load under the weight of the line. This is best described as moving your arm and then slamming on the brakes. If you let your wrist move or your arm inch forward you will weaken your cast and remove energy from the fly line. This is often the biggest problem that anglers have to overcome to achieve a better cast.

The Grip

There are two schools of thought about how to properly grip a rod. One recommends that you place your thumb on top of the grip and forward with your fingers wrapped around the rod grip. The second school suggests that you place your index finger on top of the grip pointing forward so that the rod goes where you point. Selecting the best method, however, hearkens back to the concept that no two humans are alike. Try both styles and see which one works best for you. Then you'll know the proper grip.

Right-handed anglers will want to cast with their right hand and manage the line with their left. As you soon learn, casting is actually a two-handed effort. Practice and experiment until you find a style that works well for you.

When it comes to the force applied in gripping the fly rod, the concept that less is better should apply.

Flyfishing schools are held across the nation, including the Orvis school in this Coeur d'Alene resort in Idaho. This school offers a videotaped casting critique and fishing trip, plus you can try new rods and reels.

▶ Casting is about rhythm and proper timing. Casting has little to do with strength.

▶ Correctly moving and stopping the rod creates a good cast.

▶ You'll need only a small amount of energy to move the line a short distance and more energy to move the line a long distance. The greater the distance you want the line to move and span, the more you'll have to move the fly rod across an arc to generate more rod energy.

▶ Proper stopping of the rod and

DOUBLE HAUL CASTING

With a double haul, the cast can be greatly lengthened, as when wading or in a headwind.

While you should grip the rod firmly enough to retain control, there's no reason to choke a rod grip and place it in a white-knuckled death lock with your hand. If you feel tired and experience hand fatigue after casting for a brief period, you're probably gripping the rod too tightly. Relax your hand and you'll also be able to feel more of the sensations that the rod and fly line are conveying to you. Fly rods are not very heavy so a light grip is all you need to maintain control. Many models of fly rods are sensitive enough so that you can feel your line bumping along on the bottom of the stream or feel the vibration when a fish takes the fly.

The Casting Arc

Attend a casting clinic and you'll hear the comments "from 10 to 2," or "from 11 to 1," being uttered by instructors. These are points on the face of an imaginary clock where the instructor is telling you that the rod should stop to complete a movement through a casting arc. Your head and shoulders would be at 12 o'clock on this arc.

One of the best ways to visualize the arc and the resulting movement of fly line is to mark a straight, 10-foot-long line on a clean, smooth-surfaced floor. You'll find these lines already in place in a gym floor, but you can use masking tape to create your own marks in many office buildings and building lobbies. Rig up your rod, extend up to 20 feet of fly line and place the rod tip down on the floor and on the line. Stand a rod's length to one side of the line and trace the line with the tip of the rod. (If you're right-handed, the line will work best for this demonstration if it is to your right as you face one end of the line.)

By moving the rod tip along the line, you'll discover two things: How the arc of the rod moves the fly line and how little effort is needed to shift a large length of line. Pay close attention to the back cast. Flick your wrist lightly and see how much this action is trans-

TIP:

A Rigid Wrist
One reason that good casts go bad is that when your wrist moves, the rod and the rod tip travels back, forward or lower than it should. If you keep having this problem, try tucking the end of your fly rod into the cuff of a long sleeve shirt at your wrist. You might have to move your hand forward on the rod grip, but you'll soon observe the reason why keeping your wrist locked solid is important.

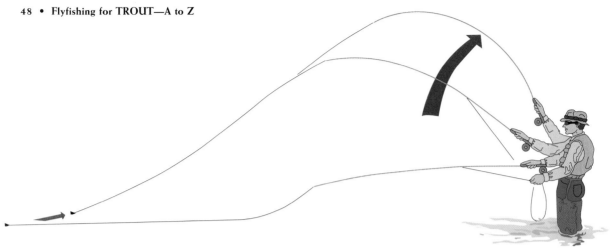

OVERHEAD CAST

1 **With your elbow close to your body begin the back cast by slowly lifting the line from the water with a strong but smooth movement. Sweep the rod up and to the rear along an arc.**

formed into raw rod energy and how it moves line. You should be able to feel the rod load and move line. Good casting arcs result in tight casting loops and better control of the fly line for better fly placement near your target. If you move the tip of the rod off the line, you will notice that the fly line begins to sag and go in unintended places in your casting area. It's

important to stay on the plane when casting.

Now you're ready to do the same movements at waist level. You will probably want to do this outside on a calm day. After you complete an arc while side casting, drop the rod tip and see how much, and where, the fly line moved after you moved your arm and the rod.

2 **Accelerate the cast until your rod hand is nearly vertical. Wait till the line is lifted and stretched out behind you.**

Once you are comfortable with side casts, lift the rod tip upward until it is extended about 6 inches to a foot away from an imaginary line extended straight up from the outer edge of your shoulder. Fly rods and lines do not pass directly over your head when you cast. They pass by on a plane slightly to your side. Before you practice overhead casts, consider donning a hat and eye protection. Even though no hook is attached to your tippet, you can still get hit in the face with line. This will also properly condition you to always wear a hat and eyewear while fishing.

One problem frequently encountered by beginning anglers who are learning to cast is incomplete follow-through after the cast. If you see line pooling up on the water—or on your lawn—a short distance in front of you, you have dropped the rod tip or failed to follow through on a cast.

An extremely useful exercise is to videotape your casting efforts. Try partnering with a fishing buddy and tape each other as you make practice casts. You'll be able to observe and record your progress and spot any problems with your presentation. Many of the top fly casting schools regularly video their students to help analyze their efforts.

TIP:

Aim High

Unless you are fighting a strong wind, never aim your line and fly directly at the spot on the water where you want it to drop. Instead, aim above the target—directly out in front of you at eye level—and then let the line, leader and tippet, with fly attached, gently drop onto the water and uncoil before you. This will spook less fish and look more natural from their underwater viewpoint.

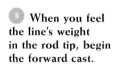

3 **When you feel the line's weight in the rod tip, begin the forward cast.**

4 **Drive the rod forward along a near vertical plane. The casting elbow should lead the rod. The line now rolls forward over the rod tip sending line and fly toward the target.**

PARACHUTE CAST

As the rod descends, stop it at an oblique angle to the surface. Jerk the rod back slightly to cause the leader and fly to land on the water after the line. This cast allows the fly to drift without drag.

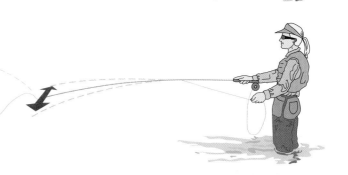

SERPENTINE CAST

On the forward cast, move the rod tip back and forth rapidly parallel to the surface. The line will form curves as it lands and the fly will float evenly without drag for a longer time.

False Casts

When you're actually fishing on a stream or lake, you cannot possibly raise, back cast, and then forward cast your line and fly to every intended target. False casts—moving the line through the air to reposition it behind or ahead of you—are the methods used to reposition your line. False casts are a necessary part of casting, and can also help remove moisture from a dry fly. On the downside, the more time that your line and fly are in the air flying around overhead, the less time that you're actually fishing. Use false casts sparingly.

The Loops

Fly line normally travels through the air in a loop. Excess line begins passing the fly line that has stopped near the rod's tip, creating a loop. You create a loop by changing the rod's speed and direction. Every angler strives to achieve tight loops with overhead casts. If you hear the crack of a whip, you're rushing the line and you cause a situation that can create unwanted wind knots in your line. Widening your loops will help avoid wind knots.

The more line that you are casting and moving through the air over

ROLL CAST

Use this cast where there is no room to back cast. Lift the rod vertically so that the line hangs in a curve beside the angler. Cast forward with a rapid whip action. To lengthen the cast, pull out more line and repeat the roll.

the water, the longer you'll need to pause to allow time for the line to completely unwind. Lightweight fly line can stay aloft for a long time, as you'll soon discover. Remember that the more fly line that you have out beyond the rod tip, more movement of your arm becomes necessary to transfer energy through the rod to move the line.

As you cast, pick an imaginary spot in the air about head high over the water where you wish to place your tippet and the fly. When your fly line extends before you and the loop uncoils, gently lower the rod tip. Lowering too fast can remove energy from your line and cause the line to drop in a pile on the water. You can also change the angle of your back cast, and stay on a level overhead plane, to avoid shooting an energized line into the water and spooking a fish.

Special Stream Conditions

You'll soon learn that trout waters have perils for your fly line and best casting efforts. Overhead limbs can suddenly move and grab your line—or so it seems. On some streams vegetation may be too tight to permit overhead casting, but suppose that you can see a trout actively feeding ahead of you, and it's a big trout. There are other ways to move your fly line and position the fly into the trout's feeding lane.

A roll cast is one method. To execute a roll cast, raise the rod tip until it is extended straight above your shoulder. Let the fly line lie on the water and loosely hang down from the tip of the rod. Next, forcefully

TIP:

Winds of Change
Windy conditions are a fly anglers worst possible casting conditions. Strong winds can push lightweight fly lines in unintended directions. This is a big problem when fishing in the West. You can try fishing at dawn and dusk when winds seem to be absent or calm. Sometimes moving up or down the river by 100 yards or so can place you in a location without wind. If it's too blustery to cast, go to the local fly shop and visit. They'll be happy to see you!

MENDING CAST

This cast stops flies from dragging when current curves the line. Shift the fly line upstream without moving the fly by lifting the line with a short flipping action.

and rapidly thrust the rod down in front of you until it is parallel with the water surface. This motion is much like delivering a karate chop down until your hand and forearm are parallel with the ground. You'll see the loop created in your line go rolling out in front of you until the line will be fully extended. You can direct the loop by moving the rod tip in the direction where you want it to go. The roll cast is easy to perfect and most impressive to see.

If you want to cast your fly a great distance, you'll want to master and use the double haul. In this cast you tug down on the fly line with your free hand as you raise the rod and begin a back cast. As the line passes behind you, release the line and permit it to move freely. This adds extra energy and stress to the rod that it transfers to the line. Then, as the line loop uncoils overhead and behind you, begin your forward cast. At this point you once again tug down on the line and add extra stress to the fly rod. As the line passes in front of you, release the line and permit the extra-charged fly line to pass along and out in front of

you. The double haul is the method best suited to reach out and present a fly to a distant trout. Mastering it takes some effort, but you'll find that effort well worth the trouble.

Mending

As you cast across a stream or river, numerous natural elements come to play on your fly line. These can include currents, eddies, and obstacles such as boulders and sand bars. To prevent snags and to keep your fly moving naturally, you'll need to learn how to "mend" the line. This involves lifting the rod and causing the fly line to curve or shift into a new position where the fly will continue to move naturally. Most mends will look like you are playing jump rope and decided to flip the rope, or your fly line, one loop to the side. Without mending you'll soon spot your fly being dragged in an unnatural "V" ripple through the water. No trout will strike a fly under these conditions.

When should you mend? In fast-moving waters you might have to start mending as soon as your fly line rests on the water. Eddies can cause currents that run upstream instead of down. Take note of the direction and speed of the currents between you and your fly and mend accordingly. You'll know too late when you see your dry fly dive underwater like a submarine!

Learning to cast properly and effectively takes knowledge, practice and experience. Attending a casting class or clinic is the best way to gain more insight. Some fly shops have casting clinics or guest presenters. You can also visit the Federation of Fly Fishermen Web site to find one of their certified

casting instructors near you. Fishing guides are another source of knowledge. Fishing partners can also help you improve your casting if you make a backyard casting game of accurately placing a barbless fly in a bowl.

The sources of knowledge are endless for anglers wanting to learn to cast better. Many anglers find that finding time to practice is their greatest obstacle. One source recommends practicing 15 minutes a day for a month. That's a good starting guideline. When you wade into the river, you'll want to spend all of the precious time fishing.

Remember to cast to a stop!

HIGHER EDUCATION

Casting is best learned through instruction and practice. Cabela's sells several casting videos with prices that range from $20 to $45. The ones that feature noted casters and fly anglers like Joan Wulff, Lefty Kreh and Gary LaFontaine will provide valuable insight.

Fortunately, nearly every state has a flyfishing school or clinic within its borders. The Federation of Fly Fishermen, (406) 585-7592, also has certified instructors and you can contact their main office to locate an instructor near you. Orvis, (800) 239-2074 X737, hosts hundreds of schools each year from Vermont to Idaho. Many of these schools are held at premier fishing destinations and can offer valuable details about flyfishing in the region's local rivers. Some classes provide loaner gear including waders—this is a great way to test new gear before you buy.

Fishing lodges also host flyfishing schools. Some state travel and tourism offices will provide details about fishing lodges and outfitters if you want to learn and fish in a new area. Remember, be sure that you are properly licensed in the state where you'll be fishing before going out to practice after class!

An angler secures a fly to his leader on the Missouri River. Knowledge of a few basic knots is essential to successful flyfishing.

6 | Knots: Staying Connected

DAVE'S HOPPER

(Dry Fly)
Popular Sizes:
08, 10, 12
Hook Type:
3X long nymph/streamer
Thread:
Yellow 6/0
Tail:
Red deer hair with cream yarn folded over the top.
Body:
Cream yarn.
Ribbing:
Brown hackle palmered though body, trimmed short.
Wing:
Underwing of yellow deer hair, overwing of mottled turkey quill.
Legs:
Trimmed and knotted stems from yellow grizzly hackle.
Head:
Deer hair spun and trimmed into square shape. Tips are left untrimmed on top of the back of the head to form a collar.

Since the fly angler will be using an extensive assortment of backing, fly line, leaders, tippets and other lines —all of various diameters—staying connected by tying the proper knots is vital. A knot should serve several purposes: connecting two pieces of line, holding fast under pressure to keep the lines together and being simple to tie so that you can spend time fishing without having to earn an engineering degree. Anglers have needlessly struggled with knots for centuries because some knot afficionados insist that you must know how to tie hundreds of knots to go fly-fishing. Nothing could be further from the truth.

There are indeed hundreds of knots and almost as many variations of those knots. You'll find posters, books, Web sites, pamphlets, brochures and videos about tying knots. The fact is you could completely give up fishing and just tie knots with your spare time, but that would probably not be a lot of fun—at least for most individuals. If you master the world of knots, you'll qualify to earn—or teach—a Boy Scout's knot tying merit badge. I prefer to go fishing and can accomplish that with an understanding of a handful of basic knots.

To make matters worse, or better— you decide—there are now knot-tying devices to assist you. Okay, some of these will work if you spend a weekend learning to use them, and if you remember to carry the instruction booklet with you when you fish. Alternately, there are basic knots that you can commit to memory and simply refresh your skill each year before you go fly-fishing. That's the simple route.

While mastering knots might seem overwhelming to many, most knots are simple. You just twist and tug. The complications arise when you try to determine what—twists— where and when to tug. And while each knot follows a basic pattern, there can be many variations of the same knot. When you find one that works well, try to commit it to memory. Take notes and draw diagrams if you must.

There are some basic guidelines to follow to make your knots stay secure and be stronger. The first and foremost principle is to lubricate all knots and the lines with moisture—saliva, lubricant, fly floatant or water—before pulling it tight and snug to finish the process. The forces of line against line caus-

TIP:

To make knot tying easier, consider purchasing a commercial waterproof tying card that fits into your vest pocket. These cards often provide great knot tying pointers and are waterproof or laminated so that they'll last for years. They're also inexpensive.

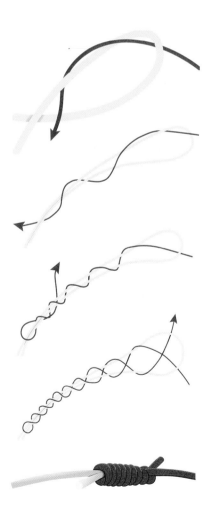

es heat and this can in some cases weaken your lines by more than 50 percent. If you use saliva, do not place the line in your mouth or you risk catching a wide assortment of waterborne illnesses. If you find that strong winds are causing stress and problems as you tie a knot, turn your back to the wind and let your body act as a wind barrier while you tie.

Pull all knots together into their finished position with smooth, constant pressure—no jerking—while tugging in opposing directions in most cases. Once a knot is seated and all wraps are in place and snug, carefully clip away the excess ends. Remember that any nick—no matter how slight—can severely weaken your main lines so cut with caution.

Another important factor as you fish is to check your knots—and all lines—regularly. Underwater rocks and other obstacles can pull on knots and untie or cut them. You'll know you have a weakness when a huge trout turns and heads away and your line snaps without slowing the trout. Then

it's too late. The following knots should help you keep things connected and enable you to land a true lunker.

Albright Knot

This knot can be used to tie the fly line to your backing material. First, form a small loop in the rear end of your fly line—most fly lines are wound on the spool with the rear accessible first. Next, pass the end of your backing line up through the loop. Make a series of wraps around the end of the fly line as it doubles onto itself and then pass the end of the backing line back down through the hole. In the Boy Scouts this is taught as the rabbit (backing) comes out of the hole, runs around the tree (your doubled fly line) five times and then dives back down the hole.

You'll need to pull this knot together carefully since the backing material is much smaller than most fly lines. The backing should bite into the soft, flexible fly line and create a bullet-like "nose" that is easy to pass through the eyes on your fly rod. On the less than desirable side, this knot can often be difficult to pass through the smallest eye on the tip of many fly rods. Hopefully, the fish that you are fighting will be large enough to make this process go effortlessly.

Arbor Knot

An Arbor knot is used to secure the backing to your reel. This is a very important knot if you fish open waters in the West and big lakes where you can sometimes fight a fish down into the backing. If the backing is not properly secured to your reel, the fish could possibly take the line away from you.

The Arbor knot is simple. Wrap the backing around your reel's axle and tie an overhand knot with the backing tied to itself. Next, tie another overhand knot in the tag end of the backing to keep the end from pulling through the first knot. Slowly pull these knots together and tighten them up against the inner axle of the reel. Note that many reels have a small groove in the spool to seat the knot and your backing line.

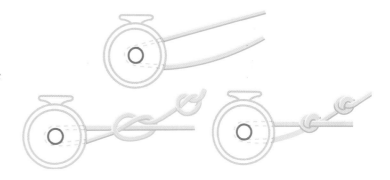

The Nail or Tube Knot

This was one of the most difficult knots I ever learned to tie while under the supervision of famed western North Carolina flytier and fly fisherman Cap Weise. Mr. Weise was the headmaster at Patterson School for Boys and taught many young anglers the finer points of fly-fishing. When a junior chapter of Trout Unlimited formed at my school, Cap Weise arrived to teach knots, fly tying and casting. I enjoyed every moment of it and wished I had fished with him more often. I frequently tie his favorite fly—the sheep fly with a muskrat fur body—in memory of him.

The nail knot is used to tie the leader butt section to the front end of the fly line. The leader will actually bite into the fly line and this forms a very compact and manageable knot. Anyway, Cap Weise had a special trick for tying the nail knot. He would keep the little stirring straw from his cup of coffee and use this as the corridor for passing the end of the leader back through.

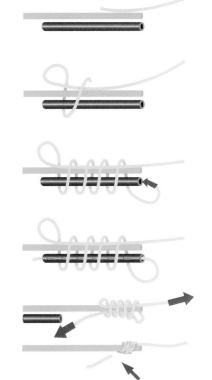

To tie this knot you place the end of the fly line and the rear of the leader overlapping each other side by side and then sandwich the small 2-inch tube piece in between the two lines. Double the leader back—forming a loop—and then wrap a series of five closely spaced wraps until you reach the end of the fly line. Next, pass the end of the leader back up through the straw and tighten the knot by withdrawing the straw along with the leader end. Pull the knot together slowly and carefully while pinching it between your thumb and two fingers. Closely trim the tag ends.

Another version of this knot that works extremely well is to carefully insert a needle into the center of the first ½ to ⅜ inch of the fly line starting at the butt end. Be sure to leave the eye of the needle sticking out of the line. Wrap the leader around the needle and fly line as described above and thread the end of the leader through the eye of the needle. Pull the needle and leader through the tunnel formed in the fly line and tighten the knot. You'll have a more compact and slimmer knot that will easily pass through the eyes on your fly rod. You can also place a drop of ™Super glue or head cement here to make passage through the eyes easier and smoother.

Loop to Loop

Many anglers have found the nail and Albright knots too difficult and time consuming. Anglers who like to switch leaders often will find that many leaders are sold with permanent loops built into the butt end. Also, many fly lines come with a loop built into the forward end of the line. You can also purchase a braided loop connector to place on the end of a standard fly line if the loop is absent. This braided loop works much like the old Chinese straw finger cuffs—when you pull, it tightens.

To connect a loop to another loop, place the fly line loop inside of the leader loop, and then pull the smaller end of the leader down through the fly line loop. When seated, these interlocking knots look like a clove hitch. This knot is easy to untie and the loops are flexible and pass through eyes smoothly.

If your leader does not have a loop, you can tie a loop in the butt end by looping it and then tying a sim-

ple overhand. Remember to moisten the line since you are working with very stiff monofilament in most cases. The smaller you can make these loops, the less likely they will snag on underwater obstacles, roots, and other unforeseen line grabbing prongs.

The Leader to Tippet Connection

This connection seems to cause many anglers the most frustration. Here you're working with fine leader material and spider web-like tippets. Most anglers find these difficult to see and feel—especially anglers more than 40 years old.

When you should tie new tippet onto a leader is a personal preference. Remember that heavy leaders can cause ripples in the water that spook trout. Having a leader that is too short or too stiff can also affect your casting abilities. In many cases tippet material helps extend the life of your more expensive leader, and tippets are normally extremely thin to avoid detection by keen-eyed trout. Use new tippet material

often. It's affordable and a fresh, flexible, and lively tippet can help increase your catch rate.

Double Surgeon's Knot

This knot is very strong and durable, and simple to tie if you are not working with very long sections of line. It is perfect for tying a tippet to the leader. To tie the double surgeon's knot, place the tippet end alongside the end of the leader with the tag ends facing in opposite directions. Simply make a loop using both lines and pass the leader and tippet ends through the loop to tie an overhand knot. Pull all four ends slowly and evenly to tighten the knot. Trim the tag ends closely and carefully.

Note that a Surgeon's Loop can be tied into a leader or tippet section by doubling the line on itself, then tying two overhand loops with the loop of the line passing through the openings that you create. This is a strong knot for loop-to-loop leader and fly line connections also.

TIP:

Leaders, tippets and fly line can be damaged by sunlight. Never hang your fly rod and reel in the rear window in a gun rack.

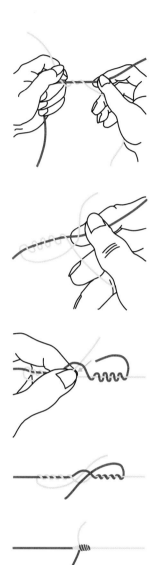

Blood Knot

This knot—for a tippet to leader connection—lies flat and is essentially formed by tying two lines onto each other in mirror patterns. It can be frustrating to tie unless you take your time. To begin, place the two opposing lines together and wrap one free end (tippet) around the leader in a series of three to five twists and insert the end through the loop formed by the two lines. Next, wrap the second (leader) line around the tippet for three to five wraps. Pass the tag end of the leader back through the same loop where the first tag was passed. You should have two tag ends passing through a loop in the center of a series of twists. The tag ends should be pointing in opposite directions. Pull the knot together carefully and trim away the excess on the tags.

Tippet to Hook Eye

When you find a knot—or a variation of a knot—that works well for you at this connection, stick with it. This is probably your most important knot in the connection.

Before you begin to tie this, check the fly and ensure that the eye is fully open to permit the tippet to

pass through. If not, use a needle to clean it out. Some snippets have a built-in needle to assist with this process. Do not use a knife blade to open the hook eye or you could cut your fingers, or worse, you could damage the head thread wrappings of the fly and cause it to unravel. If you have a hard time focusing on the hook and eye, consider using a flip-down magnifying glass that attaches to the brim of your hat. It also helps to gently push back any hackle or hair so that you can see through the eye. Unfortunately, many tiers run out of space and wrap on a bulky fly head and nearly cover the eye.

Clinch Knot

This knot is the simplest of all to tie. Pass the tippet up through the eye from below, twist the tag end of the line around itself for five wraps, and pass the tag end back through the small loop formed in

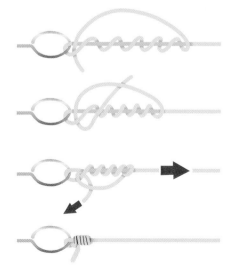

front of the eye where you began the wraps. Pinch the wraps between two fingers as you tighten the knot up to the eye. If you switch flies, you'll use this knot so often that you could tie it blindfolded.

Trimming away excess at the tippet-to-eye connection is important because any loose ends of line might be rejected by a fish as unnatural. Excess line can also cause the fly to lie on the water incorrectly and alert fish.

Duncan (Uni) Loop

This knot connects the fly to the tippet and is best remembered as tying a loop of tippet onto your tippet. First, insert about 7 or 8 inches of the tippet through the hook's eye. With the end of the tippet parallel to the standing line, turn the tippet back to create a small loop. Lay one side of the loop back against the tippet running to the

eye, and make a series of five wraps with the tag end with each wrap passing through the loop that you created. Slowly pull the knot together and then slide it up to the eye. You'll see this knot in stores on pre-tied baits and plugs intended for anglers who use clips and swivels to connect lures to line. It's sturdy but slightly complicated to tie.

TIP:

Old lines of all types should be properly disposed of in a wastebasket. Some tackle shops collect monofilament and turn it in for recycling. Never toss old fly line, leaders or tippet material into a stream or in a parking lot where it can trap and kill birds or wildlife.

Hats and sunglasses are important to help you see trout more easily and to protect your head and eyes from the elements and stray hooks.

7 Gear Up

**FLASHBACK
SCUD**

(Nymph)
Popular Sizes:
12, 14, 16
Hook Type:
*Short-shank curved
nymph*
Thread:
Olive 6/0
Body:
*Mixed gray/olive
synthetic dubbing, rough.
Pearlescent Mylar pulled
over the top and bound
in place with the ribbing.*
Ribbing:
Fine monofilamant (6X)
Notes:
*Pick out dubbing under
shank to imitate legs.*

Fly anglers have a strong common factor that binds them together and makes them unique among outdoors recreation enthusiasts—a penchant for gear. You'll see fly anglers along streams, rivers and lakes wearing bulging vests with a wide assortment of gear attached dangling from multiple cords and lanyards. This gear serves a wide assortment of purposes. Whatever amount of gear you accumulate, remember that all of the stuff you purchase should have a single purpose—to help you catch a fish.

Outfitted from Head to Toe

HATS

Hats serve several purposes. They protect your head from errant hooks and sunburn, and they possibly help prevent skin cancer. Hats can also shade your eyes and help you see into the water to detect fish. And, most important, a hat can provide cooling shade in hot weather, or help your body retain heat and keep you warm when it's cold outside.

All hats will provide some protection from hooks. Each year a percentage of anglers arrive in hospital emergency rooms across North America with a fly embedded somewhere in their head. Removing these can be a simple tug or require surgery. You should always wear a hat when fishing—period.

Hats can also protect you from sunburn and possible skin cancer. While ball caps shade your face and nose, the more traditional Indiana Jones type hat also shades your ears and neck. These hats became very popular with fly fishermen after the movie *A River Runs Through It*. On a hot summer day you can dip the hat in the river and place it on your head. The evaporation will help keep you much cooler.

The shadow over your face cast by a hat brim can help cut down the fish spooking glare caused by oils in the skin. A shadow cast over your face can also help you see into the water and possibly spot a trout. Glare can also be the by-product of many styles of glasses. You should make every effort to avoid glares near your eyes. On windy days you also might consider securing your hat with an adjustable chinstrap.

The final word on hats: Many anglers take great pride in the hat they wear, and the best rule is to buy one and wear it any and all times that you are fishing. If it's a stylish hat, I'm sure that the fish and your fellow anglers will enjoy seeing you with it on.

EYEWEAR

There are more styles of eyeglasses for fly fishers to consider than there are rods and reels combined. Like a hat, you should always wear eyewear for protection. A misguided or wind-driven hook could pierce your eye and result in missed fishing time or permanent blindness.

All eyewear that you select should be polarized. This drastically

cuts the top-water glare and can help you see rocks, snags and fish. Consider spending the extra money to buy a keeper strap. This is especially true for anglers who are nearsighted or farsighted and remove their glasses to see objects better that are near or far. Many optometrists can create custom sport glasses that match a prescription. The less time you spend fumbling with glasses, the more time you can be casting and fishing. This will also reduce the chances of dropping the glasses into the water and losing or damaging them.

When considering eyewear, take a look at the models with inter-changeable lenses. I have a pair that includes polarized, yellow and clear lenses. The polarized are great on sunny days, the clear are great at dawn and dusk and the yellow tinted lenses are perfect for cloudy and dark days. Eye fatigue can give you a headache and cut your fishing trip short. Choose a color that will keep your eyes comfortable.

There are other options to consider. Some anglers swear by wraparound style sunglasses with either solid blinders or mini-windows built in at the point where the earpiece and front frames meet. While these features can reduce annoying glare, the trade-off seems to be that they produce a tunnel vision effect for some anglers. The additional side obstruction can block ventilation and occasionally make your eyes sweaty under the right conditions and this can be annoying.

Another popular eyewear item with anglers that have passed the 40-plus-age threshold is a flip-up and flip-down magnifier that clips to the brim of a hat. These lightweight wonders can help you see the very tiny eye of a midge hook and help you inspect knots. They are available in many styles and magnification power with prices ranging from $10 to $25.

For any glasses that you purchase, consider buying a case and cleaning cloth. Some modern coated lenses are soft and easily scratched. The sand on a stream bottom has a mysterious way of making contact with your lenses and leaving a telltale scratch. Protect your investment.

VESTS

No fly angler is complete without a vest. A good vest provides pockets for stashing gear along with being a status symbol on many waters. Things to consider when seeking a vest include a solid or mesh back, the color, exterior material or shell, rear loops and the number and size of front pockets. You'll find many

vest options and one to fit your budget and preferences.

In past years, the solid green, heavy canvas fly-fishing vest was the only style available. These could be uncomfortable and hot. They were also difficult to clean and were frequently worn a few seasons until they became saturated with perspiration, dirt and oil and were then tossed. That's not the case today. If you are looking for additional warmth, consider a vest with solid back and shoulders. These vests are constructed with Lycra, Supplex, or poly-cotton blend, can help retain body heat and will help keep you warm in winter and on cool days. For summer fly-fishing, I

find that the mesh back and shoulders style vest will help keep me 10 to 15 degrees cooler and more comfortable. These vests are also lighter weight. The downside is that mesh is easier to snag on thorny brush and stray hooks.

Color options now include brown, green, tan and camouflage. Choose the one that best blends in with the background terrain where you'll be fishing. Trout can see colors and will spook when they see a dark object moving overhead. Most vests have multiple front pockets in many sizes. Some pockets zip, others snap and some are secured with Velcro closures. If you select one with zippers, be certain it is not a metal zipper that will rust. If the pockets snap or button, will the snap rust and can it be opened with one hand? Your rod will occupy your other hand so easy access to a pocket's contents

Accessories to carry flies and fishing gear range from simple chest packs with harnesses to full-sized vests with multiple pockets to hold lots of gear.

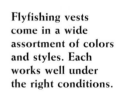

Flyfishing vests come in a wide assortment of colors and styles. Each works well under the right conditions.

becomes a priority when you're standing waist deep in rushing water. Extras on a vest like D-loops and a channel to cover the ends of your forceps will help you keep your gear handy and secure.

Many anglers like the fishing vests with large rear pockets. These are handy for storing lunch, a water bottle and a rain suit. I store my rod sock in mine while I fish. When seeking a vest to wear and use, you'll also notice shortie vests. These are popular with float tubers and can be handy if you wade deeper rivers. They have limited storage capacity, however, and you'll often pay more for less vest.

Another vest option includes inflatable models that automatically inflate when a sensor becomes wet. This could be a lifesaver in some situations, and believe it or not, every year fly fishermen drown while fishing. Rivers are full of deep

holes and moss-slick rocks and a fall could place your head in contact with a boulder. Another option are SOS Sospenders, inflatable suspenders recently approved by the U.S. Coast Guard. The price is offset by the life they save, which could be yours.

Following a new angling trend, many fly fishermen are breaking away from the use of vests completely. You'll notice that more and more anglers are wearing fanny packs or chest packs. These leave your shoulders less encumbered and can make casting easier in some cases. Some packs can hold as much gear as a vest, and some styles permit you to add storage compartments and exterior options. Be prepared to pay more than you would, however, for a fishing vest. If you still need more storage room or will be traveling to the backcountry and need to pack more gear, consider a daypack. You'll find several models designed with anglers in mind. Some packs have additional attachments to hold fishing gear and other accessories. Just remember that anything protruding from a pack will be more likely to snag on brush if you must hike thin ribbon trails to reach your angling destination. Pack colors and material rival the selection you'll find with regular vests.

An even better option today, however, is to use the newer foam patches with ripple shelves cut into the patch surface. The foam displaces water and your flies can be easily removed. This material is also becoming more popular in fly

THE PATCH

One noticeable symbol of a flyfishing vest in years past was the rectangular or round patch of wool that adorned its shoulder. Anglers placed wet flies in the patch to dry while they continued fishing. These wool wonders had a dark side, however, they held moisture and increased the opportunity for rust to destroy the hook. This resulted in a duller hook point and less chance to hook a trout. Some patches did such a good job of holding flies that you had to use pliers to extract them. Many modern patches are made of synthetic wools that work more efficiently.

Waders are vital in cold, fast-moving water.

boxes. You can buy these foam fly patches with a keeper pin on the back and apply them to any vest.

For traditionalists who like to wear their flies on their hat, you can put a patch there. Flies stuck into a canvas or straw hat generally remain there forever. I've also noticed that tree limbs are more likely to remove a fly from a hatband than from the front of a vest. Maybe that's why fly shops still sell those hats!

WADERS
While some fishermen use boats and canoes to keep dry, waders are the fly fishermen's method of avoiding water—and incidentally of avoiding leeches in some waters. Wader material choices include: rubberized canvas or cotton, breathable lined nylon and neoprene. The days of rubber-coated nylon or cotton waders are short. Consumers now demand lighter, more comfortable waders and the fishing industry has responded with Gore-Tex lined or similar breathable materials.

The first breathable waders to appear on the market had problems. They were very expensive, tore easily and tended to leak at the seams, but current versions have eliminated those problems. You'll find boot-foot—with a wading shoe permanently attached—and sock-style waders that require the additional purchase a wading boot or sandal. Experiment with the footwear to see which style works best for you. Some breathable waders are now as comfortable to wear as a pair of jeans. I've seen guides in Alaska wear

WADER CARE

It always amazes me how an angler can spend $300 on quality waders and then abuse them. After wearing the waders all day, perspiration tends to accumulate inside regardless of the construction material. You'll notice that your socks tend to feel damp after wearing any wader for a few hours. If you store your waders wet, this moisture can cause molds and odors that will attract bugs while blocking human contact.

This fly fisherman is wearing wading cuffs to keep gravel out of his boots and extend the life of his breathable waders.

them all day over fleece pants with the tops turned down. Expect to pay from $150 to beyond $300 for quality breathable waders. Most styles include a waist belt and the tops can be rolled down and the waders worn like pants, then rolled up and secured with a shoulder harness when you encounter deeper water. Other construction details to look for include reinforced knees, draw cords, removable suspenders and a storage bag.

If you want to fish during the frigid winter months, or if you chill easily, you might be better served by neoprene waders. Think of these as armor for anglers. While the 3mm-thick neoprene waders are supple and flexible, the 5mm and thicker waders will practically stand on their own. They will, however, keep you warmer and keep frigid water well away from your skin. Brown, green and camouflage are the most popular and widely available color options. There's good news for kids and ladies who like to fly-fish. Many manufacturers now make waders that are cut to fit a lady's anatomy or in smaller sizes for kids. While the size is smaller, however, the prices tend to run about the same

as those for a full-sized adult.

When you are wearing waders in the water, you should always wear a waist belt. Even excellent swimmers have drowned when their waders filled with water. A waist belt can keep your waders from filling with water and trap air around your legs and ankles to turn your waders into a life preserver. Trust me, water filled waders are like an anchor and can be very difficult to remove if you are underwater. Always use a belt so that you will live to fish another day.

One accessory that can dramatically extend the life of your waders is cuffs. These inexpensive wonders keep sand and small sharp pebbles from entering the tops of your boots. Sand and pebbles have a tendency to work their way down into the sides of your boots where they cut the thread and material in waders and cause leaks or other damage. Inexpensive cuffs—most are made of neoprene—can extend the life of your waders by years.

Follow the manufacturer's recommendations for wader cleaning and maintenance. You can also turn most waders inside out and wipe them with a damp sponge to clean them. After wearing waders, and when there is any moisture inside, hang the waders on a hanger and leave them fully extended and exposed to air to dry for a few days. Look for a sturdy hanger with slots in the arms to help secure the wader's suspenders system in place. Take care of your wader investment. You and your fellow anglers will be glad that you did.

WADING BOOTS, SHOES AND SANDALS

Let's face it, river rocks tend to be slicker than greased glass. Sand and grit in moving water polishes those rocks to a slickness that requires additional efforts on your part for traction. Add a coating of algae or muck and without firm footing, you're going in!

Felt-soled wading boots or footwear can help you get a grip on submerged river rocks. When the

felt wears out, you can glue on another layer with an inexpensive kit that most well-stocked fly shops carry. You'll still find rubber-soled waders and wading boots available but it's buyer beware if you spend much time fishing in rushing rivers and try to use anything but felt-soled footwear. The standard rubber bottoms, however, work fine in sandy bottom lakes.

The construction material options for wading boot exterior shells include nylon, leather, canvas and synthetic materials. Many boots now incorporate an abrasion resistant guard-layer on the toes

and sides. You can add this benefit to the wading boots that you currently own by buying a bottle of Shoe Goo with an applicator and applying this to the exterior of your boots. Use tape to mask the contours of where you want the application to end to create a more professional looking job and neater presentation.

When it's time to wear the wading boots, your options for security are normally laces or Velcro straps. Laces help you gain a comfortable fit and they take time to tie. Velcro can be quicker to secure but sand can sometimes interfere with the contact. Wading boots with drain holes built in near the soles can help reduce the amount of water you're lugging around and make your fishing trip longer and less tiring. You get what you pay for and quality demands a higher price in wading boots.

What about the waders with boots permanently built in? Okay, when you have your waders, you'll have your boots and there's less chance of leaving an important item in camp or at home. The wader and built-in boot combo, however, can sometimes rip or leak at the seam in poorer quality models. The bond of thin, flexible wader material where it meets a more rigid and thicker material has been an issue through the ages. If you buy

TIP:

When temperatures and humidity rise, especially in the East, many summertime fly anglers like to wet wade. This can help you stay cool and fish longer. When I wet wade I prefer to wear wading boots with felt bottoms to improve traction and protect my ankles.

this style of wader, be careful how you fold and store them to increase their life.

While wading shoes and sandals have their place, you'll find a trout stream and most rivers are not that place. You need padding and support for your ankles and the waders and sandals do not provide this support. Leave the wading shoes and sandals for saltwater or lakewear.

Winter fly-fishing presents another problem—icy conditions. For icy streams and very slick stream rocks, you might have to resort to chains. There are affordable chains with a harness system that can be adjusted to fit over the bottom and sides of most wading boots. While they add nominal weight to your feet, they can drastically increase your traction. One downside is that the chains sometimes become tangled with limbs and other stream debris.

WADER SOCKS

A fact of life: Those rocks in the river are turned to smaller rocks and sand by the water that passes over and around them. That sand and the smaller rocks will find their way into your wading boots and can then cut a hole in your waders. Neoprene socks get my nod as one of the greatest fishing inventions of all times. These socks can drastically increase the life of your waders while adding a layer of cushioning from rocks and stream

Avoid wearing thin cotton socks in waders. Wear thick socks that wick moisture away from your skin while providing additional padding for your feet and ankles.

obstacles that want to bruise your feet. When you decide to buy these, take your waders and your boots along to the store to make sure that everything is compatible and will fit comfortably. Cramping your toes in the tip of a boot can have you hobbling before you get in much fishing time.

Some socks have built-in rock guards or cuffs that roll down over the tips of your wading boots to reduce the sand and rocks that can enter your boot. If your socks do not, consider buying the cuffs separately. The more money that you save on waders and footwear, the more you can spend on fishing trips.

WADING STAFF

Falls can occur at anytime while you're fishing in and around water. Wet rocks are slippery by design. A case in point: I was going to fish a new river in western North Carolina and hiked about 100 yards from my truck down to the river's edge. The large gray granite boulder at the end of the trail was steep and moistened by a tiny, trickling spring that cried tears of water down the face of the rock. After studying the footing situation briefly, I took a step and started sliding and falling. I never recovered until I fell into the deep, cold watery pool about 8 feet below. When I made contact with the bottom, I stuck my arm out to soften the landing blow but the extreme force of the impact pushed my upper arm out of its socket.

After I made it to shore, I was hurting. I managed to tuck my wrist into the buttoned front of my shirt and find my way back to my truck. It was several hours before I completed the long drive from the remote region to the regional hospital, and the real pain began when they attempted to pull my arm back into its socket. Luckily I did not break my fly rod in that fall, and even better, it was not my casting arm that was injured! I never made a cast that day and had not rigged up my rod, which was luck on my part.

A wading staff could have helped prevent that fall by giving me an additional point of contact and some support to lean on. I never go fishing without one now. Wading staffs are worth their weight in gold and can help you reach water that you'd normally skip because you cannot wade out to reach it. A rule of thumb, however, is to never wade into water that makes you uncomfortable or causes you to panic. Some anglers go under each year because they waded into water that was beyond their skill level.

A wading staff also can be used to remove snakes from the trail and to bend tree limbs when it's time to recover a fly. This beats breaking the tip off a $500 fly rod.

There are three styles of wading staff: solid, folding and collapsible. Solid ones are hard to pack and even harder to transport in a vehicle. On the bonus side, however, they are very sturdy. A folding staff can be packed in your vest pocket and used when you need more support. A compact, collapsible type staff is a good compromise.

I have a Stoney Point walking stick that has been around the world with me. It has a comfortable foam handle that can be securely gripped when wet, collapses down to a nice, compact size, opens and locks into place securely, and can be used as a camera support. It is also lightweight and affordable.

BINOCULARS

Why would anyone want to carry a binocular on a fishing trip, you ask? Well, to discover more of the world around you in a more efficient and thorough manner.

Case in point. I was in Montana on the Missouri River and scouting for a future fishing trip. I saw an angler flyfishing about 100 yards upriver from my location. I also heard splashing down below me and whipped out my binocular to see trout feeding at the edge of a wide cover of deep foam at the near edge of the pool. I could tell that the trout were frantically surface feeding on small tan flies as they came to the edge of the foam before departure. Below me was the most active spot to fish on the river at that time and I was willing to share this news with the angler who was upriver. When I motioned for the angler to come down to me, he only waved back.

I finally got in my car, drove around the corner, and walked down the bank and told him what I saw, what he should tie on and where he should go immediately. He asked, "How did you spot those from up on that hill at the parking lot?" I showed my binocular and he said that he would never think about carrying one, until now.

There are other things that you can determine with a binocular besides discovering actively feeding trout. I can scout for trails—and dangers as I work my way upstream on a river or along a lake, and I read road and trailhead signs to determine boundaries and other posted information—without having to wade across a river to determine what's being provided. A binocular can be used to scan large sections of a river to spot feeding fish—or fish that are lying in wait behind a boulder—if you climb up and look down.

One of the other frequently overlooked practices is people watching. You don't have to walk a mile to see if that's your buddy fishing down below, you can just take a close look with the binocular. And if someone near you catches a huge trout, I'm sure you'd like to see what fly he or she is using. Why waste time by wading down to ask questions when you can look and determine for yourself?

Today your optical choices are many. Many quality pocket-sized binoculars sold today are lightweight and sturdy. Some mid-sized binoculars are also much lighter in weight thanks to modern manufacturing processes. Stick with the brand names such as Bushnell, Swarovski, Kahles, Leupold, Brunton, Nikon, Alpen, and others and you can't go wrong. Swarovski has a lightweight binocular that weighs less than 8 ounces. And yes, all those companies offer waterproof models in case you were wondering.

In recent years some companies have started producing a binocular and digital camera built into one unit. Pentax's Digibino is an example. This binocular will easily fit in a short pocket, is affordable and becomes a digital camera when you catch a trophy fish. You can also hook the camera/binocular up to your computer and e-mail an image to your fishing friends. A camera is another must-have item to pack along so that you can back up your fish tales with proof. Many record-keeping organizations request a picture of you with the fish. You can buy inexpensive and water-proof disposable cameras at many locations.

Okay, and if you're not catching fish and become tired, take a break and birdwatch. If you see birds feeding on insects at the water, the break is over. It's time to fish!

OTHER GEAR

In addition to the other mentioned gear, there are other items that can increase your comfort and keep you fishing longer. A packable rain suit is tops on the list. When you see clouds, or when the weatherman says that rain is possible, pack one along. No reason to risk hypothermia over a few fish.

Gloves are another big item that can increase comfort when winter fishing or on a chilly early spring morning. Neoprene and Seal Skin types work great. Rag wool and fleece gloves will keep you warm, but once a barbed hook makes contact with those materials, you'll have to whip out your pocket knife and cut the hook free.

A vest gets my nod when it's time to also turn up the body heat. A fleece vest worn under a wading jacket can help keep your core body much warmer while leaving your arms free to catch and land fish.

One other item, a bandana, should be taken on your trips. It can be worn to keep the sun off your neck, can be dunked and worn damp to keep you cool on a hot summer day, and can even become a sling or rope should you have a medical emergency.

A newer version of the wet bandana is a wrap around neck cooler that you dunk in the water. The inner layer has a material that absorbs water and delivers enhanced evaporation and body coolness. These are more expensive than a bandana and they work.

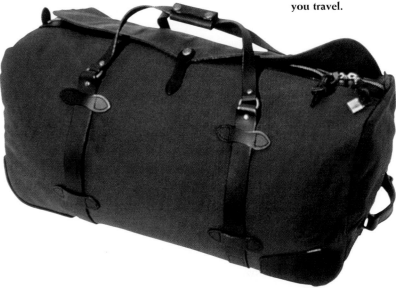

A large wheeled duffle bag is useful for hauling gear when you travel.

HARD BODY ANT

(Dry Fly)
Popular Sizes:
10, 12, 14, 16, 18
Additional Colors:
Brown, black
Hook Type:
Big eye dry fly, straight eye
Thread:
black 6/0
Body:
Balls of brown or black epoxy at front and rear of hook shank.
Hackle:
Black, in middle of shank.
Notes:
The balls are formed by adding paint to the epoxy when it is being mixed and are then appiled to the hook. The hook should be rotated until the epoxy balls are dry, then the hackle is applied.

ON THE MOVE

If you buy all the aforementioned fly-fishing gear, you'll need something to store it in when you travel. I find that a travel bag helps keep flyfishing gear together so that nothing is left behind when you have to dash off on a short notice invitation to go fly-fishing. You'll discover that waders, boots, a vest, net, fly boxes, rain suits and all that other "necessary" gear create a rather large pile of goods. A small overnight bag will not hold it all. There is a solution.

Large rolling duffle bags are one option and these work great for moving through airports when you have to fly to reach your fishing destination. Several companies, such as Orvis, G. Loomis and Cabela's, all make versions of these bags with prices starting at around $100.

You'll also discover mid-sized bags that will hold reels and your fly-fishing vest, and others with special mesh or vented compartments to hold wet waders and boots. A word of caution: Airlines panic if you have a bag with something dripping out of it. Allow enough time for the water to dry from your waders or clothing before you pack and board the plane. In recent months large hooks, forceps and other fly-fishing gear have been banned from carry-on luggage. You'll have to check the rules, but I recommend always keeping your reels in your carry-on. Even with today's stringent airline regulations, baggage can go into a black hole never to return to the real owner. And since all bags must remain unlocked, the number of missing valuables is skyrocketing. So much for ultimate airline security.

One thing's for certain, keeping your fly-fishing gear stored in one location, with the most common items prepacked in a travel bag, can make the mad dash to head out the door less hectic. The end result is that you'll be on your way sooner and possibly gain more minutes in your life to fish. Somewhere out there are the right bags to help you accomplish this organizational task. Good luck in your search for the bag(s).

FISHING GEAR

Once you've covered your body, it's time to focus on gear that will help you rig up, cast and handle fish better. The more efficient and productive you are, the more time you'll have to fish. This increases your chances of actually catching something.

NETS

Fly fishermen are often depicted in artwork standing in a river with a fly rod tucked under one arm while the other arm is outstretched. In the extended hand is a net—normally a wooden one—with the fish partially captured. Nets are fly-fishing icons and in recent years expensive nets—there are many—have become popular status symbols.

A search at any fly shop or sporting goods store—plus the catalog retail fly shops—will reveal many nets in many styles. Options include teardrop shape nets, elongated ovals, triangles and collapsible nets with a flexible metal band that can be collapsed and stored in a pouch that's worn on your belt. Net handles and base are normally constructed with aluminum or wood. Cherry wood, ash, walnut or bird's eye maple are popular wood choices. Expect to pay a premium price for premium woods and construction.

There are two styles of netting material used in net—a large open mesh and a smaller fine mesh with holes about the diameter of a pencil. Some anglers express concern that the more open mesh can permit a fish's fin to pass through and ultimately damage the fish. This could be true, if you're not careful. Opt for the smaller mesh if you are concerned about this. I use the finer nets because I can also use the net to capture streamside insects and mayflies that are washing by in the water when I want to take a closer look at insects.

Net handles are available in lengths ranging from approximately 6 inches to larger boat nets that can be more than 4 feet long. The longer nets should be limited to boat use because they, as a rule, are too cumbersome to carry streamside.

There are also accessories for nets. One is a fine micromesh seine that attaches to the base of the net handle and opens into the net to create an instant seine. Another accessory is a retractable ruler that is easily pulled out when you have a fish in your net and want to measure it. Other options include nets with folding handles and a wide

BUILD YOUR OWN NET

There's a way you can have a custom flyfishing net at a fraction of the cost of the upscale models—build your own. Instead of paying $100 for wooden net, you can purchase a kit from several sources, like Cabela's, and then build your own net. The process will take several hours and makes a great winter project. Most kits include the wooden frame, net material and lacing to secure the

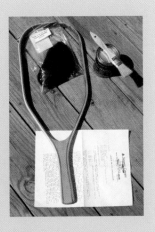

net to the frame. You must provide your own wood finish and a needle to lace the netting onto the wooden frame edge. Follow the instructions to achieve the best results.

The process:

Sand and inspect the wooden frame for splinters. This is a good time to write your name and other information on the net handle or frame. You can also buy decals, such as a fly or fish image, at some fly shops if you want to customize your net and add a touch of class. Next, apply several coats of varnish. Sand the finish between coats if necessary to remove any bubbles and hardened bumps or drips of varnish or urethane. Use a sharp nail or small drill bit to open any net lacing holes should they become clogged with the varnish.

APPLY VARNISH

After the varnish has dried completely, thread the needle with the lacing thread and begin sewing the net to the frame opening. Tie a sturdy and secure knot when you have completed the lacing process. Attach any loop or clip that was provided to the end of the handle. You now have a custom net that you can be proud of. Go fishing and try the net out!

SEW NET TO FRAME OPENING

ATTACH LOOPS OR CLIPS TO HANDLE

Creels can help keep fish fresh should you decide to keep some of your catch.

vest, buy a sturdy retractor.

You should try to inscribe your name and address in your net. This might help with gear recovery if it falls over the edge of a float tube or should fall from your back while you are leaving a fishing area. I know honest anglers who have found and returned nets. I know other anglers who have lost cherished nets and this ruined an otherwise great fishing trip. An address can often help bring the owner and the finder together.

assortment of net attachment systems. Some attachment systems are magnet to metal and are easy to separate when you're trying to land a fish. Others require you to reach back to unsnap a two-pronged release like miniature spring-loaded pliers. Experiment to see which system works well for you.

Some nets arrive with elastic cords attached to the base of the handle. I've seen anglers loop this through the D-ring on the back of their vest at the base of the collar. When you're walking through brush, however, the net can become entangled and the cord stretches. At the moment of truth when you discover that you're snagged, the net can break free and fly at you. A better option is a retractable net-keeper. I like the sturdy one built by Gear Keeper. A net can become heavy when it's wet so, if you are going to attach your net to your

CREELS

Should you decide to keep a fish, you'll need somewhere to store it. Creels are the answer. There are models made like wicker baskets with leather shoulder straps and canvas models with webbed shoulder straps. Some canvas models have measuring lines printed on the side and numerous storage pockets built into the outside.

Where legal, consider gathering leaves or a handful of grass. Wet this material, and place it in the creel with your fish. Evaporation will work to keep your trout cooler and fresher. You can also dip canvas creels into the water to enhance their fish-keeping qualities.

Any and all creels should be thoroughly cleaned when you return home or to camp and should be completely dry before being stored. This will reduce odors and keep the creel serviceable longer.

KETCHUM RELEASE

This small hand-held prod has an opened tube section on the front

that slips over your leader and tippet to slide down the line into the fish's mouth. You simply thrust forward and the tube encloses the fly and backs the hook out. These can be much faster to use than forceps. Currently there are two sizes. These gadgets are also great for forcefully and carefully removing flies and hooks from overhead limbs and vegetation. Other anglers have reported that they work well when you are trying to remove a fly that's lodged underwater and you can't see the fly but you can follow the fly line down to it.

THERMOMETER

Trout like certain water temperatures, and individual species live in specific temperature zones. You'll find brook trout in colder water at higher elevations, rainbows in the next temperature zone and browns more tolerant of the warmer waters at lower elevations. A thermometer can measure the water temperature.

In the spring, rising water temperatures can predict insect hatches and determine when a big hatch might start. It's a good idea to take the water temperature and log it into your fishing journal to reveal patterns at your favorite fishing spots.

FORCEPS
Forceps and pliers have stood the test of time with anglers to recover swallowed or deeply embedded hooks. You'll find that there are numerous styles and lengths available in exchange for your dollars. If you buy forceps that lock together near the finger rings, you can secure them to the outside of your vest where they're readily available when a trout is on the end of your line. A new style of forceps has a small tube opening on the end that you slide down your line and into the fish's mouth and over the hook so that you can simply push and remove the hook. No more gripping and twisting the hook that stresses the fish and can damage your expensive fly.

Forceps come in shiny chrome, gold and flat black. The flat black models are less likely to alert fish to your presence. I spray-painted mine—originally shiny silver—black.

Any and all forceps should be anchored to your vest with a short piece of string or to a retractor pin. When forceps or any gear goes underwater, this generally means that it's gone forever.

CLIPS OR NIPPERS
When fly-fishing, you'll need a way to efficiently trim excess line after you tie a knot or adjust a tippet length. I've seen anglers place the line in their mouth and bite it in halves. Hmm, a dentist told me that

the newer and sturdier high-tech lines could wear a groove in tooth enamel if you fished regularly. A more serious possibility is exposing yourself to giardia and other waterborne illnesses. The solution is clippers.

Standard fingernail clippers work well and most models have a hole in the base so that you can tie this to a string and then anchor it to your vest. Many well-designed nippers incorporate a small sharp point or spike for opening fly eyes that might have head cement stuck in there. Other models have knot-tying aids, hook disgorgers and other add-ons. Any unit that you select should be easy to use when your hands are wet and should be large enough that you can hold it securely. You can also use many of these clippers as scissors if you need to trim the wings on flies. This does a much better job than a pocketknife. Some nippers can be

expensive. You should always secure it with a retractor or you run a high risk of losing it.

FLOATANT HOLDER

In recent years there have been holders designed to keep floatant handy when you need it. One model is soft rubber that grips the base of the plastic floatant bottle, while another a mini pocket that holds the entire bottle of floatant. Either system works well but be certain to place the floatant so that you can see how much goo comes out when you squeeze the bottle.

HOOK SHARPENER

There are several styles of hook sharpeners. Many have small grooves that you slide the tip of the hook down. Another popular one is a mini triangular sharpening stone made by Gatco. One edge has a groove for points, and this compact unit can be used to sharpen knives.

LANYARDS

If you really like gadgets, then maybe a lanyard is the solution to help you keep them organized. These rope loops are worn around your neck and serve as a base for holding a wide assortment of items. While they can help you keep items organized and handy, I some-

Storing leaders and tippet in see-through bags or wallets will help you stay organized, avoid tangles and protect the lines from nicks.

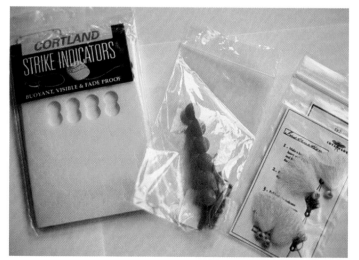

times find that the lanyard can become entangled in brush when you're crawling through thickets. If you buy one, consider a model with a foam neck pad and a clip that will anchor the lanyard to the front of your vest or shorts. You'll be glad that you did.

RETRACTORS AND GEAR KEEPERS

A problem with a fly-fishing vest and an assortment of gear is that the gear is clipped close to your vest when you might need to use it at arm's length. This includes nets, nippers, walking staffs and forceps or Ketchum release. A retractor is the solution.

Most of these small self-winding devices permit you to pull an item out to arm's length. Then the thin metal cable retracts into the small clip-on housing when you're finished with the item. There are many models and styles.

You'll want to find one with a sturdy base clip that secures it to your vest. Some models of Gear Keeper have nuts and bolts to fasten the unit to a large D-ring loop. These are normally sturdy enough to handle a net and walking staff.

The standard rings and spools will easily hold nippers or floatant. Some models will hold and release two items. If you go for cute, then consider the one that's designed like a mini fly reel.

You can also find keepers that use a magnet and steel base for quick removal without a cable. These are easy to disconnect but can be a little difficult to reconnect when attached to the rear of your vest and out of sight.

LEADER WALLET

When I first saw one of these I was skeptical. Now, however, I believe that this item can help you stay organized and protect your leaders. No more random stuffing of leaders into a pocket where they instantly turn into a tangled bird's nest. A leader wallet can keep them coiled separately and will protect the leader from sharp edges and sunlight. A wallet is also easy to handle when you're in the water and trying to find the right leader without having to wade a long distance back to shore to complete the task.

LEADER STRAIGHTENERS

After extended storage on a reel or in a leader wallet, memory sets in and some leaders coil like a rattlesnake when you want to use them. A leader straightener can help heat the line and reduce the coils as you pass the leader

TIP:

Leader wallets are useful for separating leaders that you plan to change and store in your vest. A wallet will also keep the leader from being nicked and weakened by sharp objects in your vest pockets. Without a wallet you'll soon have a tangled nest of line built up in your pockets.

between layers of leather or rubber. Some argue that this can weaken leaders. You'll have to be the judge at how much pressure to use and how often. If your leader is coiled and too stubborn to use, maybe you're not fishing often enough!

FLY BOXES

You'll soon discover that you cannot have too many fly boxes. You'll want to set up a box for nymphs, dry flies, streamers, salmon flies, bugs and grasshoppers and for other circumstances that you could encounter at various times of the year and in different regions. Your choices for fly boxes include hard plastic exterior shells in clear and colors and foam or metal (aluminum or pointed steel) exteriors. Boxes can have multiple chambers, open ribbed or with foam pads or specially designed grooves to hold various sizes of flies. The prices for the boxes can range from a few dollars to $100.

Foam-lined boxes seem to be receiving the popular nod from anglers at this time. They are light, sturdy and the foam does not hold moisture like some other materials do. The smaller, clear multi-compartment boxes are also popular because you can see what's inside without having to guess what's behind each mini door. Some fly shops sell small versions of these with the shop's name, address and phone number on the lid. These are sometimes collected as memorabilia of all the places or states in which the angler has fished.

I counted more than three dozen fly box models in one catalog. Some are designed to catch anglers and buyers while others are designed to hold flies safe and secure. A fly box should not hold a fly in a position that damages hackle or body material. Remember also that the box should fit in at least one of your vest pockets. Shop wisely.

For the ultimate box, sometimes at substantial savings, consider buying a preloaded fly box with an assortment of flies already inserted into the box. These can be very helpful when traveling and you seek to use flies that are currently productive in a particular locale.

KNOT-TYING AIDS

The splicing or joining of fly line to leader and leader to tippet can be frustrating at times. Whether it's stinging sweat in your eyes or a hoard of mosquitoes and gnats, being able to see the line and pay attention to a knot-tying process can become a challenge. Luckily there are knot-tying aids that can make the process go faster and smoother.

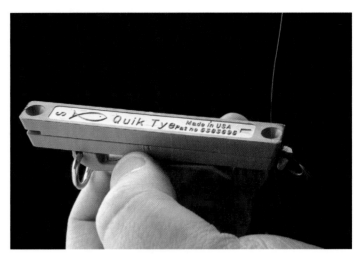

Be forewarned that it will take some time, patience and a bit of practice to learn to master these knot-tying devices. Once you master them, however, most become second nature. These can be a boon on windy days when grasping and holding line becomes more of a challenge. Most knot-tying aids are small enough to easily fit in a vest pocket, are lightweight and will provide years of dependable service.

PACKABLE RAIN SUIT

If you remember the old thick rubber rain suits, you remember that you got wet either from rain or sweat while wearing them. There was no comfort in them. Rubber-coated nylon suits were a little better but ripped easily. Both suits tended to be bulky, hot and difficult to pack.

Today anglers can find affordable rain suits that are very packable. Most have a nylon or Cordura exterior, roll up smaller than a pair of jeans and will keep you dry.

Look for suits with brand-name breathable vapor barriers such as Gore-Tex or Dri-Plus when possible. Good rain suits should have a hood, adjustable cuffs, draw cord closures, and pockets. The suit should permit flexibility so that you can comfortably cast.

Another option to beat spring showers is a wading jacket. Some styles of these angling-friendly coats double as a rain jacket and are comfortable enough to wear all day. The prices for some coats, however, are as much as you'd pay for an entire breathable rain suit. Again, shop wisely.

WATER BOTTLE AND FILTRATION SYSTEM

Water, water everywhere and nothing to drink. That's the way you'll feel after a few hours wading a spring creek or when fishing from a float tube in a high-mountain trout lake. At no time should you consider drinking from a spring or small stream. The health risks are too great today. I don't care how many times that water runs over rocks—according to an old wive's tale—if it's outside, it's not safe to drink.

Your option is to pack water or filter it. For packing water, you'll want a water bottle or hydration system. Some daypacks now have a soft bladder enclosed in the pack with a hose that runs across your shoulder to deliver an instant drink. Talk about convenience, this is the ultimate. One of the reasons you can have a headache after a few hours of fishing is dehydration. In the summer this is more common. Drink up and drink often.

If you use the water bottle system, find a size that fits into a vest pocket or that can snap onto your wading belt. You'll want the heavy water bottle to stay in a location where it does not interfere with casting and does not jab you in the back and cause discomfort.

If you want to travel light, there are now compact and lightweight systems that permit you to filter water. Some are attached to water bottles and others are pumps. Some of these can be expensive and you'll need to read the fine print to determine what is filtered out. Consider quality names like PUR when facing the choices.

HEADLAMP

Some of the most prolific hatches on a trout-filled river occur at dawn and dusk. This is also the time when many anglers, unfortunately, are waiting for the sun to rise or dashing to the trailhead or parking lot to avoid darkness. A headlamp can make night navigation easier. The strap on headlamps will stay in place, leave your hands free and can put out a lot of light for such a small unit.

Another option is a small light that clips onto your hat or vest.

Some of these units have flexible heads so you can turn the light where you most need it. Many of these mini units are smaller than a pack of cigarettes.

Another reason for having a headlamp is to explore night fishing. If you know your fishing area well, this can be a productive time to fish. Some huge trout become nearly nocturnal and prowl the rivers and lake after the mass of anglers has gone home. You can at least bet that the crowds will be absent if you fish at night.

RIDE THE WAVE

No mention of fishing gear would be complete without providing some details about float tubes and pontoon boats. These have sharply grown in popularity in recent years. You can use them on moderate rivers and reach almost all the water and shoreline in any lake. Before you leave shore, you should always wear a personal flotation device (PFD).

Float tubes are available as round donut-shaped floats or open ended "U"s or horseshoes. You'll need fins to paddle and maneuver the float tube along. Some models are as comfortable to sit in as a Lazy Boy recliner. The starting price on these is about $100. One bonus is that these "boats" can be packed and carried on trips. I frequently pack

mine along on trips where I must fly to reach my destination. The fins are dropped in the bag along with a small pump.

Pontoon boats—a seat perched between two long floatation tubes—have made their way onto rivers everywhere. The operator can sit high to see around and cast easier. Oars are used to paddle the boat along or to change position. Most of these pontoon boats will help you cover a lot of water. Follow the manufacturer's recommendations about navigating rough water and waterfalls. On the downside, pontoons can be big and bulky. You'll need a pickup truck or trailer to take them to the water and the huge fixed frame platform makes them nearly impossible to take along on a flight. Some places rent them so maybe that will help you solve your dilemma. See pages 126 through 131 on float tubes and pontoon boats for more details.

The magnificent rainbow trout, a native of the North American Pacific slopes, has been introduced into streams, rivers, and lakes throughout the world.

8 | *Know Thy Trout*

HARE'S EAR

(Nymph)
Popular Sizes:
08, 10, 12, 14, 16, 18, 20
Hook Type:
Heavy wet/nymph
Thread:
black 6/0
Tail:
Pheasant tail fibers, hare's mask guard hairs, tuft of hare's mask fur, Red Fox squirrel tail, partridge hackle fibers, brown hackle fibers or none
Abdomen:
Rough dubbed hare's ear/mask
Wingcase:
Pheasant tail fibers, bronze turkey tail or wing, gray goose or duck, white tip turkey tail, peacock herl or pearl flashabou
Thorax:
Dubbed hare's ear/mask
Ribbing:
Gold tinsel, fine oval tinsel or fine gold wire
Legs:
Rough dubbing or guard hairs

One of the most interesting facts about trout is that these fish like cold clean water. Trout live in pristine mountain streams, rivers and lakes. The presence of trout reveals that the water is about as pure as you'll ever discover or wade in. The presence of trout also points to temperature ranges normally below 70 degrees Fahrenheit on the thermometer. One of the strongest characteristics of trout is their preference for cold waters. Those waters are often rippling through the most scenic lands in North America. Perhaps the inspiring and breathtaking scenery is why so many anglers take up the fly rod and pursue trout.

It may also be because trout are so colorful. You'll never meet a fish as colorful as the brook trout with its olive back, orange and white fins and purplish and blue hues. Or how about the rainbow trout: with a stunning stripe of red swiped along its side in stark contrast to the fish's shimmering silver, this is a regal fish. Then there's the brown trout with its colorful spots contrasting against a tan and gold background. And don't overlook the golden trout with its gold hues and the cutthroat with its brilliant red gill cover. Yes, trout are colorful indeed, and the colors are so vibrant when you pull a trout to your hand and see it on the end of the tippet.

And there are those that proclaim that trout taste delicious. Others argue that trout present a distinct angling challenge where a misplaced fly line can send a minute but unnatural ripple across the water's surface and cause a weary trout to seek shelter and avoid all flies for the remainder of the day. Yes, trout are tasty and elusive, which only adds to their widespread public appeal.

The trout fishing industry is a multibillion-dollar business in North America. Factor in guides, outfitters, lodges, rods, reels, other equipment, travel and numerous other factors that put anglers on the water and you can hear the cash registers ringing often and loudly. Then there are the hatcheries, biologists, and others who manage the other side of the industry. Lots of folks support trout with their wallets, and their occupations and conversely, many families depend on the future survival and prosperity of trout in North America.

BROOK TROUT

Trailhead kiosks and signs along the rivers will let you know special flyfishing regulations and trout creel limits for the waters. Learn the rules before you fish to avoid a situation.

Trout are members of the family Salmonidae. This group is salmonids and includes salmon, graylings and whitefish. All species of salmonids provide excellent table fare, but the trend these days leans heavily toward catch-and-release. When properly performed, this unselfish act provides future fishing opportunities for you and other anglers.

Trout fishing with a fly rod gives you a chance to experience the great outdoors. Flyfishing demands that you slow down and observe the small details of the natural world around you. Roaring highway traffic gives way to roaring waterfalls and the sounds of nature.

Whatever your reason for going trout fishing, it's always a special occasion when you can stare a trout in the eye and see its wildness staring back at you.

So which trout will you meet on your next outing?

Brook Trout

Brook trout, or *Salvelinus fontinalis*, have a characteristic and prominent white leading edge along their fins. Brook trout are actually a member of the char family. The brookies, as they are often called, have a body with a dark olive background that is spotted with lighter spots with a bluish tint and a series of vermiculations, or random squiggly wormlike lines, running across the back.

Brook trout territory in North America ranges from northern Georgia up into the far reaches of northern Canada, and as far west as Iowa. Brookies have been introduced into some western states and in other countries, like New Zealand.

Habitat for this species includes high mountain streams and lakes. Along the spine of the Appalachian Mountains, the fish can be found in narrow, darkly shaded and laurel-covered mountain streams that are frequently broken by raging waterfalls. Some of these streams are a scant 2 feet wide and maybe a foot deep in some pools, but the water is clean and clear—perfect brook trout habitat. In Maine and across New England, brook trout can be encountered in small remote lakes and in the small streams that gently flow through many of the small rural towns.

Brook trout are opportunistic feeders and will eat a wide variety of insects, fish and whatever they can find. This fish species is often easy to catch because it is always hungry and lives in areas that are noted for their lack of quality and abundant food sources. These are reasons that brook trout tend to grow slowly. Colder water temperatures result in decreased metabolism and this eventually results in less feeding activity, and less growth. Some regions have 7- or 10-inch minimum size limits on brook trout. A 12- or 14-incher will be a trophy in many waters. Farther north in Canada the brookies are often much larger.

Brook trout spawn in the fall and the eggs develop with fry emerging in the spring. In recent decades, unfortunately, this fish has shown a drastic population decline in many areas. Pollution and development are often the causes of demise, with acid rain playing a role in some regions of the Appalachian Mountains. Stocking efforts have not helped. Stocked brook trout are less colorful and less likely to survive in wild conditions because these factory fish seem to be less survival oriented unlike a true wild-strain brookie that can be very skittish. Brook trout can be found in some mountain lakes but are known to avoid deep waters. In some areas brook trout are referred to as "specks" or "speckled trout." These should not be confused with the saltwater speckled trout—or weakfish—found along the Atlantic coast.

Handouts, such as the one below provided by an Idaho fishing club, can help identify trout species and clarify local catch limits and prohibitions.

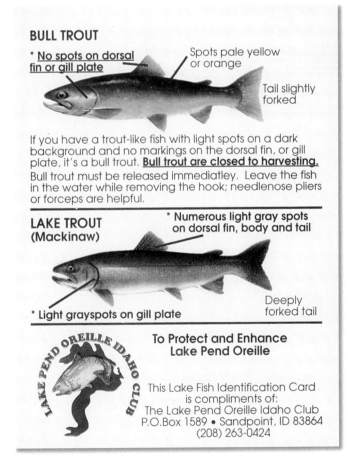

BULL TROUT

* No spots on dorsal fin or gill plate

Spots pale yellow or orange

Tail slightly forked

If you have a trout-like fish with light spots on a dark background and no markings on the dorsal fin, or gill plate, it's a bull trout. **Bull trout are closed to harvesting.** Bull trout must be released immediatley. Leave the fish in the water while removing the hook; needlenose pliers or forceps are helpful.

LAKE TROUT (Mackinaw)

* Numerous light gray spots on dorsal fin, body and tail

Deeply forked tail

* Light grayspots on gill plate

To Protect and Enhance Lake Pend Oreille

This Lake Fish Identification Card is compliments of: The Lake Pend Oreille Idaho Club P.O.Box 1589 • Sandpoint, ID 83864 (208) 263-0424

There's hope for brookies. A recent ban on removing brook trout from the waters of the Great Smoky Mountains National Park on the North Carolina and Tennessee border is showing promising results. To help the native brook trout defend their territory against encroaching fish, the native brookies were removed, and the streams were treated with a chemical to kill all fish, including rainbows and brown trout that readily prey on smaller brook trout and compete with them for food. Fish barriers were installed to keep rainbow and brown trout from returning to the headwaters and the brook trout were reintroduced. Initial reports are that this expensive and multi-year project is resulting in more trout per mile in the revived waters. Only time will tell if the brook trout survives in its lower range reaches.

Brown Trout

Brown trout ruled the waterways in Europe for decades before they were released into American waters. Browns (*Salmo trutta*) were first imported into America around 1880. By the mid-1880s browns were released in rivers and streams throughout the Atlantic states region and, a short time later, the nonnative trout made their way to the Rocky Mountain states and beyond. The following years were filled with angler anger in some areas as the brown trout began to crowd out native fishes. Browns often proved harder to catch and this added to angler rage.

Brown trout have an erratic pattern of darker (black and red) spots against a light tan background. Most of the spots will have a slight, light-colored halo around them. A true identifying characteristic is that a brown trout's tail will be free of any spots. Browns grow to be the largest-sized trout in North America. A nearly 40-pound brown trout was caught in Arkansas on the White River in 1988.

Brown trout spawn in and near November in much of North America. The available food supply and water quality determines how rapidly a fish grows, matures and dies. In streams with limited

BROWN TROUT

RAINBOW TROUT

food sources it is common to catch a brown with a large head and seemingly smaller body. The size of the head indicates this is a mature fish, but the stunted body means available food sources are far and few between.

In a brown trout's early years, it feeds entirely on insects—and lots of them. The fish species is known for having a voracious appetite. As the fish grows larger (12 inches and beyond), it turns its attention to crayfish and then to other fish. Crayfish patterns are very popular with brown trout pursuers, especially anglers who focus on landing the larger fish. Brown trout generally grow larger and out-compete other trout species in the waters where they compete for food sources.

Browns prefer water temperatures between 55 and 65 degrees Fahrenheit but can tolerate temperatures as high as 80 degrees. You'll often encounter browns in the more open waters of silted meandering river bottoms, and especially in meandering grassy meadow streams where the water is general-ly shallower and warmer. These can be ideal casting waters since there are few, if any, trees to snag lines and flies. Brown trout also do well in lakes and some browns move out of the lake into tributaries, as is often the case in the fall on the Brule River in northern Wisconsin.

Don't let a brown trout's size, appetite and shallow haunts fool you. This fish species is recognized as being hard to catch and, in some cases, where there is a lot of fishing pressure, the larger trout sometimes become nocturnal in nature. If you like hard-fighting fish that can grow larger, however, then the brown trout is waiting for your best efforts.

Rainbows

When trout are discussed, the rainbow is the species most fly fishermen are familiar with. In recent years the species underwent a name change to *Oncorhynchus mykiss*. Rainbows are noted for their pattern of many solid black spots that spread from their nose, across their

YOUNG TROUT TRAITS

Young trout have a series of dark oblong bars along their sides. These bars, or parr markings, can be used to determine the type of trout. In some species the parr markings disappear soon after the fish starts growing in length, and in other species the markings remain into adulthood.

back and out to the tip of their tail. If you catch a fish and it looks as if it has been heavily peppered, you probably have a rainbow in your hand. If the trout also has a distinct red- or pink-hued stripe along its sides, a dark olive upper back and reddish fins, it's probably a rainbow. Lake dwelling rainbow trout, however, are often less colorful and can be a dull silver color.

Rainbow trout were originally native to the Pacific slope regions of North America. They were carried eastward and released, and in recent years they have been transported and successfully stocked worldwide. Rainbow trout can now be caught in Europe, where ironically, they compete with brown trout for territory and food.

Colorful rainbow trout are like all species of trout and seek clear, clean water that's well oxygenated. Much of the dissolved oxygen comes from waterfalls often found in trout streams and rivers. Rainbows prefer streams, rivers and lakes with rocky bottoms. Warm waters release oxygen and cease to be ideal trout habitat. Rainbows find 55 to 70 degrees Fahrenheit ideal and can tolerate water temperatures as high as 80 degrees for short periods of time. Summer droughts can often take a toll on rainbow trout populations, as

is often the case in the Rocky Mountain states.

Rainbow trout, unlike the other trout species, spawn in the spring. This is often the reason cited by some states for having fishing seasons closed during a few spring months. A mature rainbow female—often called a hen—can lay several thousand eggs in a redd —a hollow scooped out in the sand or gravel by the spawning fish. In about a month the eggs mature, the fry absorb the bulging yolk, and the fry set out on their own. Life as a small trout is fraught with many perils and survival rates can be low in many areas.

Rainbows feed largely on insects, and sometimes on other fish. You'll often find rainbow trout feeding during the middle of the day. This fish species is very popular with anglers everywhere that it is found, which includes most states other than Florida, Mississippi and Louisiana. Rainbow trout are often stocked in the tailraces below dams, and seasonally released into cold lakes. These trout can grow large.

Steelhead

One of the fastest ways to start an argument with trout enthusiasts is to call a steelhead a rainbow, or state that rainbow trout are non-migratory while steelheads migrate. Steelhead trout are a species of rainbow trout that are generally known for migrating out of lakes and up into tributaries. Steelheads are rainbow trout that migrate long distances.

Because of the amount of time spent in deep, dark lake waters, steelhead are often more silvery in color (think of aluminum foil in some cases) and have a faint stripe along their sides. The rainbow's pronounced black spots—an identifying trait—are also faint and smaller on steelheads. Steelhead, however, undergo a color change during spawning season and the females and males can have pink or red gill covers and more colorful stripes along the sides. Spawning seasons normally range from the end of November until the first of July, depending upon the waterway.

Steelheads, like the rainbows they are, were originally West Coast residents. Enterprising anglers transported the fish—or eggs—to the East and introduced them into lakes and rivers. Today there's a thriving population in the Great Lakes and smaller lakes across the East. Spring steelhead runs bring droves of fly fishermen to the mouths of many tributaries in the lakes. Along Lake Superior's western shore in Minnesota, the steelhead can only run a short distance because of very high waterfalls—natural fish barriers—that are often less than 100 yards inland. This situation, however, does not keep the fish from running as far as they can, and often creates a large concentration of anglers.

Steelhead like to spawn in the calmer back edges of watery pools. These large trout will deposit thousands of eggs in a small redd that they wallow out in the bottom substrate. After spawning, many steelheads return downstream to the lake or ocean.

In Alaska, returning steelheads swimming upstream encounter dead salmon carcasses washing downstream. The steelheads are able to dine on decaying salmon carcasses. If you can reach Alaska in the fall, the trout fishing can be superb and the steelheads are huge. Visit King Salmon and give this a try, you'll be glad that you did. Watch for bears!

Other Trout Species

There are numerous other trout species that you will encounter in North America. Most, however, are regionally limited in distribution and sometimes even the astute fish scientist will argue about which species they are looking at. Among the other trout you'll possibly encounter are: cutthroat, golden, Gila, bull, Mexican golden

IT'S A COLORFUL WORLD

Trout are noted as being the world's most colorful fishes, and male trout can be more colorful during the breeding season. Trout colors also serve a purpose. When viewed from above, a trout's dark back helps keep it concealed from predators such as eagles. A bird will have difficulty seeing a trout's dark back against dark-colored rocks, submerged logs or other underwater structures. When viewed from below, a trout's light or silvery underside and belly sheen make it appear to blend into the sunlight shining through the water surface. A trout's speckled color scheme acts as camouflage and can help it blend into shadows and underwater structures.

A TROUT'S EYE VIEW

If you ever have the chance to don a professional-grade skin diver's face mask and go underwater and look around, you'd be amazed at the view. I did just that, along with fins and snorkel, to explore a large and deep mountain pool that I suspected held huge trout. They were there, lurking in the shadows under the ledges of the ragged boulders that jutted into the pool. Why did these huge fish never take a fly? Because they could probably easily see me when I approached the pool to cast.

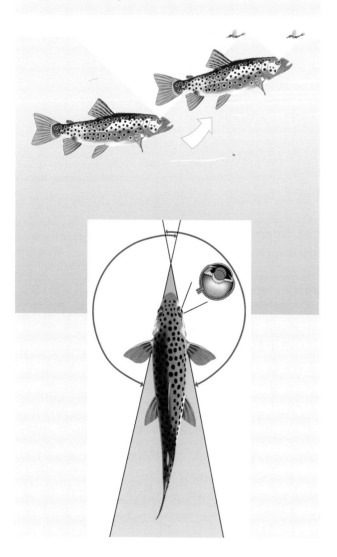

and lake. Of these, the cutthroat species probably has the largest dispersal in the Rocky Mountain states. Several of these small species of trout are of special concern, or possibly endangered in some areas, and must be returned immediately to the water if caught.

This is the case with the bull trout in Montana near Glacier National Park. The fish there are off-limits to anglers and must be returned to the water immediately. Bull trout are actually members of the char family—like the brook trout, lake trout, Dolly Varden and Arctic char—and have characteristic light spots against a dark, often olive, background. Hopefully the decline of the bull trout can be reversed. These large trout—that mainly feed on other fishes—can be found in the Northwest states including Washington, Oregon, Idaho, Montana and the northern edges of Wyoming and California.

Cutthroat trout are widely known for their characteristic red or dark burgundy hue along the lower edge of their gill plate covers. The fish often looks like it is bleeding at the throat. Explorers Lewis and Clark encountered the cutthroat on their trip across the West and one subspecies bears the explorers names in its Latin species name. Today cutthroat trout are subdivided into nearly a dozen subspecies and all reside in the mountainous West.

One of the smallest trout populations is the rare Gila trout. This fish's home range is confined to the Gila (pronounced Heel-ah) Mountains in Arizona and New Mexico. Gila trout are very golden in color and look similar to California's golden trout that shares a similar bleak future. The days might be gone when we'll ever be able to legally bring to net one of these trout.

Lake trout, as a species, are widely distributed across northern North America. These trout grow large, are confined mostly to lakes, and are silvery to dull green in color. The fish prefer deep waters and grow very slowly.

Common Trout Characteristics

Some features are common among all trout. Trout have a lateral line, or series of sensory pores along their sides that detect water movement, vibrations and help the fish avoid obstacles. An alert fish can feel you wading in the water because of vibrations caused when you move your feet. A trout can even sense—through its lateral lines—your footsteps along the stream bank or small stones displaced as you move. The fish also utilizes its well-developed inner ears to detect high-frequency vibrations and to maintain equilibrium in the water. Shout while you're along the edge of a lake and a trout will probably hear you

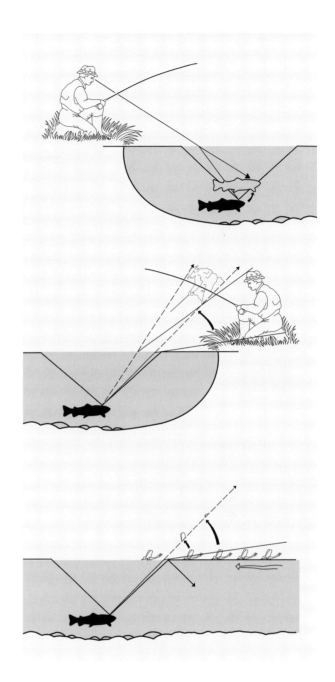

Refraction distorts the fisherman's view of the trout (top) **and allows the fish to see at a wide angle above and on the water surface** (center and bottom).

because water is an excellent conductor of sound waves.

A trout also uses the sensations received by its lateral line and inner ears to maintain its space in a school of swimming fish. These lateral lines are versatile and can also detect odors, chemicals and pheromones in the water. Trout also have taste buds in their mouth to help them discern odors and food.

In addition to the lateral line, trout have nares (our equivalent of nostrils) that help them detect odors. They use this information—carried by water currents—to locate food sources, find other fish for spawning and to avoid predators. This organ can be used to determine your presence in the river and alert trout that you are there and fishing. Oils, such as suntan lotion, and other chemicals in your clothing and on your waders can warn a trout of your presence.

HORNBERG

(Wet Fly)
Popular Sizes:
08, 10, 12
Hook Type:
3X long nymph
Thread:
Black 6/0
Body:
Flat silver tinsel
Wing:
Two yellow hackle tips inside 2 mallard flank feathers
Hackle:
Brown and grizzly mixed
Notes:
The wing is wide and tied on the side of the shank so it covers the body.

Trout have thin oval-shaped scales. The scales are smaller and thinner to help the fish move more efficiently through swift water. Growth rings on a trout's scales can sometimes be used to determine the age of the fish. A trout's scales and its protective coating of slime help prevent disease-causing organisms from entering the fish's system. That's why it's important to wet your hands before landing a trout, and when possible, quickly release the fish without handling it. Dry fingers can remove or disrupt the protective slime coat. Barbless hooks help in this effort. Fish are susceptible to numerous waterborne viruses, bacteria, fungi, protozoa such as whirling disease and parasitic worms. Life underwater can be rough!

A trout's gills separate oxygen from the water. Sand, chemicals, fish lice and human fingers placed in the wrong location can damage a trout's fragile gills and reduce its oxygen intake. A weakened fish is more susceptible to diseases.

Trout use the three single fins located on the back, anal area and tail, or caudal, to thrust through the water. The side-to-side movement of the fish also applies force against the water and helps propel the fish forward. Trout have a soft adipose fin located along their upper back positioned forward of the tail. A trout's tail is normally square in shape and can be slightly forked.

Fins help a trout move through the water to catch food and escape predators. Some fins are in pairs. The pectoral fins, on the lower and forward section of the fish, are located just behind the gill openings. The ventral fins are located near the halfway point along the lower edge of a trout's body. Trout use these paired fins for braking purposes. The ventral, or pelvic, fins can be slightly angled to cause the fish to rise or descend in the water. This works much like the dive planes of a submarine. Fins are vital fish body parts and a trout has a very high probability of dying if a fin is removed.

What keeps a trout suspended at a certain depth in the water? Trout have an internal air bladder that can be inflated and deflated to help the fish maintain buoyancy. Angled fins also keep the fish floating at its desired depth. If you grab a trout too tightly and roughly, you can damage the swim bladder. This leads to a slow and prolonged death. Take it easy when handling trout to better ensure their survival.

Trout use their vision to spot food and predators. A trout can see above, forward, below and to the side with its uniquely designed eyes. Special muscles help the fish move its eyes to see in various directions as necessary. The pupils of the eyes are oblong and a trout has rods and cones in its eyes similar to humans. Trout do not have eyelids.

Water bends light rays. Hence, when you spot a fish in the water, it's not where it appears to be. In most cases, for every foot or two of depth, the fish will be about 6 inches closer to you than it appears. This light refraction works in a trout's favor. If it is stationary in the bottom of a clear pool of water and looks up, the bent light rays help the trout look up and out in an ever widening circle beyond the water. If you see a trout in a deep pool of water, it can see you. A trout can easily spot you, particularly when you move near the water's edge on the top of a short bank.

Trout can also detect colors—thanks to rods and cones in their eyes. A trout can spot a tiny size 24 midge fly floating by overhead with ease and quickly determine if it is

PREFERRED WATER TEMPERATURE OF TROUT

BROOK TROUT
prefer water temperature ranges: 55° to 65° F.

BROWN TROUT
prefer water temperature ranges: 55° to 65° F, but can tolerate up to the mid-80's.

RAINBOW TROUT
prefer water temperature ranges: 55° to 70° F, but can tolerate up to 75°.

the right size and shape as similar insects in the area. If they can see that—an object so small that fly-tiers and anglers have trouble seeing it—they can easily see you.

Some anglers go to extreme measures to avoid a trout's view and prevent spooking the fish. Crawling on hands and knees to the edge of the pool is only the beginning. Some anglers wear total camouflage, along with a face mask, to blend in. Others wear dark clothing and wide-brimmed hats to merge with vegetation shadows. In all cases, you should avoid brightly colored clothing or a flashy hat.

Trout have upper and lower teeth. In a male trout, the lower jaw can become longer during the breeding season and form a kyte. Trout use their teeth to hold prey and do not use them to chew. Males will fight over a female during the spawn and this often involves the use of teeth. A trout also has a tongue.

Trout have many of the organs

commonly associated with humans who live on land. Trout have a heart, liver, kidneys, a spleen, intestines, a brain, testes or ovaries for reproduction and a urinary bladder. A trout's heart rate depends upon the water temperature and its activity level. In frigid, wintry water a trout's heart rate can be as low as 20 beats per minute.

Trout can become sexually active as early as one year of age, but three to four years is normal for most species. The female uses the fins on the rear of her body to create shallow gravel nests or spawning redds. The average female can lay up to 1,000 eggs and will carry rocks in her mouth to cover her eggs after spawning.

Birds that eat fish include bald eagles, great blue herons (*below*) **and pelicans.**

Temperatures Tell The Tale

Water temperature plays a key role in helping you discover where trout might be lurking. In general, all salmonids, including trout, prefer water temperatures ranging from 50 to 65 degrees. Increasing water temperatures can often increase trout activity, to a point. After water temperatures reach 70 degrees, most trout species will vacate the area and move up-stream to cooler water or go down into deep pools

with cooler springs seeping into the bottom. They can tolerate warmer temperatures for a brief period before they die.

Brook trout like the coldest water temperature ranges. If water temperatures rise above 65 degrees Fahrenheit, brook trout become stressed and begin migrating upstream to locate cold, deep pools, refreshing underground springs and shaded areas under ledges and boulders. Brown trout are more tolerant of warmer temperatures and are found in lower elevations and near sandy river bottoms where you'd never find a cold-water loving brook trout. Rainbows seem to enjoy water temperatures between these extremes.

Human activity is the most common cause of increased water temperatures and the resulting disappearance of trout. Runoff from high mountain resort parking lots, ski resorts with artificial snow, logged and clear-cut areas, takes a toll on trout by adding to the increase of local water temperature. Some farming practices, including use of agricultural chemicals, runoff of animal waste, and overgrazing stream banks, can also change water temperatures. In some areas, rising temperatures have been successfully cooled down by planting shade trees along the water and by fencing livestock out of sensitive areas. Forest fires, road building, development and dams can all work to increase water temperatures and make the conditions less than ideal for trout species.

Maps Lead to the Water

When you are seeking a place to trout fish, the best place to start your search is with a state game and fish department. Most states that have active and prospering trout populations run their trout fishing systems separately from their other game fish species programs. Most states produce booklets and maps that show stream classifications and indicate locations and access points. North Carolina, for example, has a detailed book with a half-dozen stream classifi-cations. Most classifica-tions range from catch-and-release only to no closed season or size limit restrictions. Most depart-ments now post this infor-mation on their Web sites.

There are several places that trout live. Trout lakes and ponds exist far and wide across North America. Most tend to be at higher elevations, generally above 4,000 feet, and are numerous in northern regions where winters are longer and air temperatures rarely climb above 90. Northern tier states like Maine, Vermont, Wisconsin, the Dakotas, Montana, Idaho and Washington are premi-um trout territory.

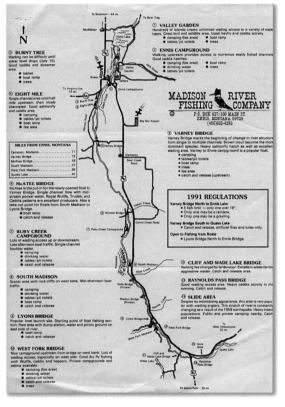

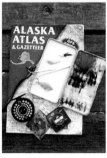

Many states provide maps indicating where the trout are located and the spe-cial regulations and limits that apply to anglers.

Alaska is a flyfishing mecca and maps like this guide map will help you find good waters and fish.

Trout streams are where most anglers will encounter trout. In some states, stocking trucks prowl the back roads and technicians and biologists pour baskets full of lively trout into the water. Much of this expensive put-and-take system is supported through the sale of spe-cial trout fishing licenses and stamps. In some states the only water cold enough for trout habitat is found at the bottom of tall hydroelectric dams. These dams are encountered from the Carolinas to California. Some tailraces offer superb trout fishing, but remember to check for pending water releases to avoid being swept away.

Where Trout Come From

The crowd gathered by the edge of the river near Bangor, Maine, turned their attention skyward as the roar of a plane engine grew louder. The small Cessna made a treetop pass over the location, banked sharply a few times, and then passed through the trees and down the river corridor directly before the crowd. From underneath fish—lots of trout to be specific—came pouring out of an opening like little bombs dropping head first into the river. The plane made a few passes, emptied its fish holding tank, and left the area. I had witnessed Maine's method of dispersing trout. This is the fastest and most efficient way for the Department of Inland Fisheries to carry fish to remote lakes.

While airborne trout stocking is controversial—some anglers argue

A HATCHERY

Entrance to White River National Fish Hatchery in Vermont.

A trout hatchery is an interesting place. Many hatcheries across the United States have closed in recent years because of funding cuts and risk of spreading whirling disease. At the White River National Fish Hatchery in Vermont you can see various stages of a trout's life. You'll see trays of trout eggs and incubator barrels and tubs, covered rearing ponds and pools of large trout. These trout will be rounded up in nets, placed in oxygenated tanks on trucks, and transported to streams, rivers or lakes. The process is controversial but the insight is educational.

Trays of fish eggs in the hatchery.

Incubator tanks for trout eggs.

that too many fish die from the shock—I checked after the operation in Maine. I could not find any floaters—dead trout—that afternoon or the next morning. I checked the river for more than a half-mile below where the fish were deposited. I did see locals who had heard of the stocking and were fishing all along the banks, many netting trout for a meal.

My next introduction to trout stocking came while I was employed by the North Carolina Wildlife Resources Commission in the western part of that state. I was invited to help the local fisheries crew stock fish. I climbed on a truck, dipped a net into the large tank with on-board oxygen generators, and scooped up nets full of trout. Next, I raced to the river to pour in the fish. This was tiring work, but very interesting.

In the past, trout have been spread across North America in unique ways. At one steep gorge in west-

ern North Carolina volunteers helped lower buckets full of trout down into the gorge by a complex system of steel cables.

In high mountain regions in the West, trout rode in barrels on horseback to reach backcountry lakes and waterways. The horses had to move fast because high temperatures and dwindling oxygen levels in the barrels quickly caused the trout to become stressed and could cause them to suffocate and die. In some western areas, forest service crews were recruited to backpack trout to backcountry lakes and headwaters.

There are other ways to move fish, as I discovered in West Virginia. An agreement between the rafting out-fitters association and the state resulted in funds to hire a helicopter. I helped load trout into barrels that were then placed in the helicopter. When my turn came to take a stocking flight, I climbed into the chopper, found my seat and

Special tents protect the trout from birds.

Trout in pools of water and raceways before being released.

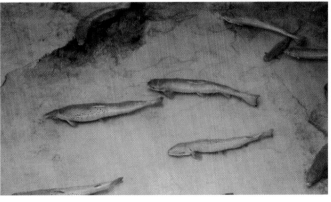

WEST VIRGINIA TROUT STOCKING VIA HELICOPTER

West Virginia's trout stocking by helicopter is an expensive process. Funding to stock trout was provided by Class IV Outfitters, the state river guide and outfitter's association, and the state's department of natural resources. Volunteers helped load and stock the fish.

Trout are transported in special trucks with oxygenated tanks (above) before being placed in special containers for the trip to the river by helicopter.

The trout are poured from the hovering helicopter into inaccessable areas of the river.

strapped myself in. A large barrel full of wildly thrashing trout was placed between my legs. Even before the chopper became airborne I had to lean over and press my chest and face over the barrel to secure the trout. In seconds the helicopter and stockers—including me—were dropping down into the deep, rocky, river gorge. A tap on my shoulder and a thumbs-up indicated it was time to release the fish. I sat up, grabbed the barrel, tilted it out of the door and began pouring trout into the river, while the chopper hovered a few feet above the water surface. The trout dove and disappeared into a deep pool of clear mountain water.

The chopper was used because there were no roads into the gorge. This was also a better way to increase fish survival rates. When we landed back in the parking lot to change stockers and load new fish, I emerged soaking wet, thanks to the splashing fish. This event also attracted a large number of anglers who hiked into the gorge and were waiting for the fish. Some were landing fish before all of them were released.

Naturally Reproducing

Not all trout fall out of airplanes or helicopters. Today, trout are naturally reproducing in much of their occupied and suitable habitat. Changes in regulations and public attitudes have made much of this possible. Brooks, browns and rainbows are reproducing across North America. Stocking has become a thing of the past in some states and regions.

Problems in a Watery World

One reason for the decline in stocking has been whirling disease. This disease attacks a fish's nervous system and causes it to spin around and around in a circle. Trout infected with whirling disease can have curved spines or be deformed in other ways. In some areas entire fish populations have been wiped out by this problem. State stocking programs—with hatchery infected fish—helped spread the disease into some waterways. Rainbow trout seem to be most affected.

Research is underway to find a cure for the problem. Do your part and thoroughly clean and disinfect your waders before moving from one river to another. There are other guidelines posted—and possibly required—in some states, so discover the requirements and follow them.

If diseases are not enough, trout in some regions face a bigger threat—human expansion and encroachment. Pollution from farms, golf courses, ski slopes, housing developments and highways all work to degrade water quality. In some states, roads and highways have been widened, streams have been straightened and habitat destroyed. What was once prime trout habitat is erased forever with a few wipes of the dozer's blade.

If you like to fish for trout, you should get involved in efforts to find a cure for diseases and battle development that unnecessarily harms trout and their habitat. Future generations of anglers will thank you for it, and so will the trout.

What would our world be without trout?

In many states, waters inhabitable by trout are stocked with hatchery raised fish. Some state authorities have ceased stocking programs due to concerns that hatchery trout might carry diseases.

Aquatic insects in trout streams often crawl onto rocks
or bushes as they begin life out of the water.

9 What Trout Eat

KAUFMANN'S STONE

(Nymph)
Popular Sizes:
02, 04, 06, 08, 10
Additional Colors:
Brown, black
Hook Type:
Curved nymph
Thread:
Brown 6/0
Tail:
Black or reddish brown goose biots
Ribbing:
Black or brown transparent Body Glass, V-Rib, or Swannundaze.
Wing:
Three segments of dark turkey tail, cut or burned to notched shape.
Abdomen:
Black or brown dubbing, rough and translucent synthetic or natural fibers.
Thorax:
Same as body.
Legs:
Dubbing picked out at thorax.
Head:
Same as body.
Other Materials:
Antennae: reddish brown or black goose biots.

Trout are well known for having a large appetite and being opportunistic feeders. While the species is generally recognized as being keenly alert and easily spooked by errant shadows and unnatural noises, trout of all species are widely known for their voracious feeding habits. In most cases, anything that falls into or on top of the water and that can be fit inside of a trout's mouth is subject to becoming trout food.

On the other side of the feeding coin, however, are the facts that trout have keen vision and often have keen super-selective feeding patterns. Flies and lures that are presented to a feeding trout must frequently be a near-perfect match to the current size, shape and color of the natural food sources that the local trout are feeding on at a given moment.

A case in point—early one summer morning I was walking the banks of a Wisconsin trout river and preparing to fish when I noticed a large number of trout actively feeding in a large deep pool behind an elbow bend in the river. My best guess was that up to 20 fish were breaking the surface, and I quickly noted that several of the trout were large—appearing to be more than 20 inches long. I was familiar with this section of the river and frequently saw large trout hiding in the corridors between clumps of watercress that grew knee-deep in the river just below this pool. Apparently some of those big trout had moved up into the pool to feed. The question was what were they so hungry for?

At first glance I could not see anything on the water. This told me that the food source was either subsurface and nearly reaching the surface in an almost completed hatch, or that something—a tiny mayfly or midge—was on the surface and getting the trout's attention. Since I was upstream, and the trout were feeding and facing upstream, I needed to determine the food source without spooking or alerting the trout to my presence.

I walked downriver to the next big hole and did not see any feeding action. I did notice a few spent Tricos—a very small insect— swirling in the edge of a small eddy. Hmm, this might explain why I could not see the food source from any distance away—unfortunately, I

A tiny Trico lands on a vehicle that's parked by a stream.

TIP:

If you see an insect in the water or on the surface, try to capture it. This is where a fine mesh landing net works wonders. To gain a better view of an insect, consider packing a small magnifying glass in your vest pocket.

the dark brown bodies of spent Tricos with their wings outstretched and flat on the water surface. No fish were feeding on them.

I looked at the point with the most fish feeding action and soon spotted a light tan mayfly with upright wings. It was gone—inhaled by a trout—before I could determine what it was. This process was repeated again and again. After I had invested a considerable amount of time watching the trout and observing the flies, I deduced that the mayflies were Tricos that were hatching. The trout must have found these to be the caviar of the insect world.

had left my binoculars in another fishing vest or I could have had an instant answer to the puzzle.

I hurried back upstream, tied on a spent Trico-pattern fly with its outstretched clear wings and knelt down on the grassy streamside up from the hole. My game plan was simple. I would cast into the head of the pool and let the fly wash into the feeding lane. I began casting, determined the distance and gently dropped the fly onto the water. No takers. I recovered and cast again only to have the same lack of activity. After a few more casts I changed flies, tying on another Trico, and repeated the process. Again, no results.

I was miffed so I decided to take a closer look. I walked near the pool, dropped to my knees and moved closer, then I crawled through the wet grass to glance over the edge and observe the fish that were still feeding. I soon noticed that the edge of an eddy was littered with

I returned upstream, squirted floatant on my Trico-pattern, and massaged the wings into an upright position to resemble the spiked hair of a radical teenager you'd see hanging out in the dark corner of a shopping mall. Numerous casts later I was still fishless, and as the sun rose higher and the air temperature increased, the trout feeding frenzy in the pool diminished. I had to know the secret so I walked down to the pool, stepped onto a sand bar and feverishly worked to capture my own Trico. When I finally landed one I saw that the body was a tan color and not the dark brown that the spent Tricos—and my pattern—exhibited. I cut my fishing trip short that day and returned home to tie Tricos—size 28—with tan body and upright wings.

The next morning I was at the same

pool when the sun rose. The fish feeding action soon heated up again, and I made the first cast. Instantly I had a fish on. In the next hour I fished the same hole and landed more than 20 trout. When I would land a trout at the front of the hole, the trout would drop back to the rear of the hole and start feeding again on Tricos that washed to them. I'd cast back there, hook another trout, and land it. The feeding would then resume at the front of the hole. Those fish with their sharp teeth wore out two flies in the process, but I had solved the mystery.

I'll not dwell on matching the hatch. The important lesson learned was that trout key on shapes and colors. When viewed from below, trout see dark patterns of winged insects passing overhead against a light or mirror-like background. Clear water can act like a magnifier to increase the size of a mayfly—or your lure—and help trout take a better look at what it sees. Size, shape, and silhouette are important. With the early morning sunlight hitting the water at a sharp angle, the fish could also possibly see glints of color which explained why they were hitting live Tricos with the tan bodies and ignoring my same-sized fly with the dark body. Color can be an important factor.

If you had to always match the hatch, anglers would not buy the very popular Royal Coachman—a flashy red fly that resembles no

insect I'm aware of. Red, however, does attract a fish's attention according to some camps. There are other patterns that do not imitate mayflies or insects found in the natural world.

When you're fishing flies—nymphs, wet flies, and streamers—subsurface color becomes more critical. You are working to gain a trout's attention—and solicit a strike—in a watery world where everything is in constant motion. In recent years more nymph patterns have begun sporting gold or copper beadheads. Flashiboo, antron and other materials have also helped tiers create flies that put more color, shimmer and rainbow spectrums before a fish. A glint or sparkle can also work to catch a fish's attention.

The best answer to the question of what local trout are feeding on, frequently involves an understanding of local insects and stream life. In early spring midges appear in many waters and freshwater shrimp become active. As the daytime air temperatures warm and more sunlight penetrates

Pine beetles will often become trout food if they fall into the water.

Crawfish

Small frogs are favorite food for trout when they can find them.

Subsurface Feeding

To effectively pursue trout, you have to gain an understanding of their underwater world. Most trout lie facing upstream and watch foods wash by beside them or float by over-head. Nearly 90 percent of the food that a trout takes is consumed while the entire fish remains underwater. While a trout can turn its fins and let the rushing water help it rise to the surface, the movement to return to the lie—or holding area—requires energy. For a fish to survive, the energy gained from consumption of a food must be greater than the energy required to consume it or the fish will perish. This is a basic principle of survival. While there's nothing wrong with being a dry fly purist, you can land more fish if you drop a fly beneath the water's surface. Fish feed there because it's more energy efficient.

There are many types of mayflies and insects that begin their life underwater as a nymph or worm much like a butterfly begins life as a caterpillar. All of these originate from eggs laid by an adult. Sometimes the eggs are laid on the water surface, and sometimes eggs are laid on streamside vegetation. In other cases the adult dives back to the bottom of a lake or river to

Feeding trout often break the water surface or will root tiny underwater insects out of in-stream vegetation.

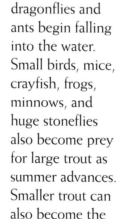

Freshwater shrimps, or scuds, are an important part of the trout diet.

the water to warm it, mayflies often begin to emerge. As summer grips the land with longer periods of daylight, grasshoppers, crickets, beetles, wasps, bees, inchworms, ladybugs, caterpillars, moths, earthworms, dragonflies and ants begin falling into the water. Small birds, mice, crayfish, frogs, minnows, and huge stoneflies also become prey for large trout as summer advances. Smaller trout can also become the target of other trout. Your options are limited only by the region's insects, crustaceans, fishes, reptiles, mammals and other natural food sources. It is important to try to mimic the size, color and action for you to be graced with a reaction from a trout. Look at the underside of any fly you tie on and determine how the profile will appear to a trout.

deposit the eggs. Life as an insect near a trout stream is wrought with peril. Anytime they are near or on the water, a trout could strike.

Two types of aquatic insects are most prominent in North America. Caddis larvae—they grow to resemble moths and butterflies—and nymphs—the early stage of a mayfly—spend their first year or two of life underwater. They often resemble small worms or flat scorpions with legs. Caddis flies in the underwater stage may construct small tubular homes from pebbles and sticks that they carry along with them much like a hermit crab with a shell. You'll readily spot these abandoned houses stuck to the sunny side of rocks when the hatch is underway and caddis nymphs emerge from their watery world. The progression from egg to adult passes through bottom dwelling larva in its stone case, the transformation into a pupa that swims to the surface with the aid of an internal air bubble, and finally an emerging adult complete with wings. The caddis completes its transformation by turning into a moth-like, egg-laying adult. In a few caddis species the adult sheds its skin underwater and swims to the surface. Trout readily eat caddis in all stages of development.

On many streams the caddis emergence occurs around the period between Easter and Mother's Day and on to the beginning of June. In a good year the hatch can be overwhelming for some anglers. When

the air and water temperature reaches is right, the swarm can be prolific. You'll have caddis flies crawling into your ears, crawling across your sunglasses, and walking up your arms and down your neck. They don't bite so don't panic.

You should, however, catch one and look at the color, shape and size. Most are tan, brown, gray or black. A caddis pattern tied on size 12 to 16 hooks will normally resemble any caddis fly. The elk hair caddis is the most widely used and performs well as a high floater. This fly is easily tracked as it rides along on the surface of the water.

These tiny flies imitate small insects found underwater.

There are many types of mayflies that hatch during specific times, or in specific regions, of the United States each year. Trout are selective in what they will eat and will pass on some mayflies as they search for others.

Shells of aquatic nymphs dot a rock by a trout stream. These insects have crawled from the water to emerge in their flying stage.

Another popular version is the tent-wing caddis. This fly frequently has quill—normally from a turkey feather—shaped like a miniature tent over its back.

One of the most prolific caddis hatches that I've ever experienced was on the Rush River in Wisconsin. There were so many flies that it seemed as if you were inhaling them with every breath. At times the swarm was so thick it looked like a scene from a horror movie. The trout, however, cherished the moment—which lasted for a two-week span—and went on a feeding frenzy. The water was one big splash for the duration of the daily hatch. Big and small fish alike focused on the caddis hatch and fed on the adults that fluttered on the surface. Several fish went

airborne to capture caddis flies that lifted off. It was spectacular, and like all good things came to an end. Most hatches of a specific color and size of insect last for about two weeks. This was true of that hatch and I fondly remembered the action each time I returned to the river during the next year.

The mayfly—there are actually hundreds of types of this species—all begin life as eggs and then become clingy nymphs that can walk and crawl along on slippery underwater rocks. If they lose their grip they'll wash downstream and possibly end up in the mouth of a trout. After a year or two of living on the bottom, a mayfly nymph swims to the surface and sheds its skin as an emerger. The new adult version—a dun—resembles a miniature sailboat with graceful wings or sails. The adult must cling to the shucked skin as its four wings dry—the two rear wings are small and often overlooked. Duns are very vulnerable to attacks from hungry trout at this stage as they drift downstream.

Duns eventually become airborne and head for cover on vegetation along the banks. They'll rest and grow here, and then shed their skin a second time to become a complete adult mayfly. Most species are yellow, gray, brown, or olive.

Adult mayflies dance into the air in swarms and mate. The female frequently returns to the water to deposit eggs and may take flight

again and will sometimes rest on streamside vegetation. For most, their above-water freedom is short lived and, after a night or two of flight, the adult drops onto the water surface and dies with wings outstretched. You can easily spot these spinners with their opaque plastic-like wings. Trout will readily eat these.

Spinner action can be short and furious. Once when I was in Vermont I noticed that the Orvis bulletin board reported rusty spinners were the ticket for action. I bought a couple of flies since I was going to go flyfishing the next morning. Here again was a local insect and pattern that I had never seen or tied, but I placed faith in the fly shop information. The next morning, shortly after dawn, I was on a small stream several miles from Manchester. When I saw a trout rise, I cast my rusty spinner ahead of it. I let the fly drift back, and promptly got a strike. I worked the trout to the riverside and quickly released it.

Something unusual soon caught my eye. In front of me in the tall weeds was a huge spider web. It was full of spinners with rusty colored bodies that had fallen during the previous night. A few were giving their parting flutters. I had not spotted any on the water, but the trout knew they were there. Several more trout enthusiastically let me know that morning that they also enjoyed rusty spinners. By 10 a.m., however, the action was over and the fish lost

interest. The spinners must have all been flushed down the river. You could not have paid a trout to bite a rusty spinner. Not only knowledge of insects is important, but being alert to changing water temperatures and its impact on local insect populations is also vital.

In early spring the water temperature may reach the magical 60- to 70-degree Fahrenheit range between 2 and 4 p.m. By midsummer the best hatches, such as the Trico action I experienced, will often occur at sunrise and sunset. You will gain some of this information with experience and you can also ask questions and get solid answers at many fly shops. Many of these establishments and their staff want to see you catch fish. They know this means more future business and a steady customer base for them.

Sometimes you must make a streamside judgment call. It's important to try and determine what trout are eating so you will know what fly to tie on. A trout might be focused on pulling a specific size spinner from the water in the morning, then switch to emergers

Fish are opportunistic feeders and will eat insects that fall into streams, like this beetle shown here in actual size.

Trout also like dragonflies.

Even large insects are subject to become a meal for a trout.

as the day progresses and the water heats up and a hatch begins. By late afternoon the feeding preference might turn again with a splash in favor of lighter-bodied duns. Stay alert to the insect life cycle as it progresses during the day and you'll have better success.

Grasshoppers are an important part of a trout's summer diet and the hopper hatches on many streams bring out anglers en masse.

When you are in doubt about what's hatching on local trout streams, visit your local flyfishing shop. Most of these specialty stores will have updated chalkboards with useful up-to-the-minute hatch information. Some of the better-equipped and advanced stores will place this information on their Web site. Bentley's Outfitters in Eden Prairie, Minnesota, is a good example. During the winter months Bentley's also invites DNR fisheries biologists to give presentations and some of the topics covered include insect life in local waterways. This is valuable information for a fly fisherman.

There are other places to learn about insect life. In recent years videos and Web sites have started providing very useful information. Watch for this information on nature programs and channels. A few serious fly fishers have enrolled in basic biology classes to learn about insects. And there are numerous very thorough and affordable books for those who like to home study in their leisure time.

The Fly Angle

Another great way to move your understanding of the trout and insect relationship forward in quantum leaps is by learning to tie your own flies. You can save money—to spend on fishing trips—and you can increase your satisfaction by catching a trout with a fly that you tied. Many fly shops teach tying courses during the slower winter months.

If you travel and fish, you can take along a basic tying kit and create a pattern to match local insects that you capture and observe. Tying flies can also help you design flies to meet your local insect population's unique characteristics. Some insect species vary with subtle regional differences. For example, golden stoneflies and black stoneflies in some western areas are large 2-inch-long insects. Stoneflies in the East, however, are about an inch long. I'll warn you that tying flies can be as much—and often more—fun than fishing, especially when the fish are not biting. Flytiers can be a quirky lot, however, so be forewarned before you get in too deep!

What Size Hook Works?

The size of hook you use to tie a fly will determine how the fly lands and sits on the water, and how a fish sees it. Nymph pattern hooks are often thicker and heavier. The additional weight helps pull the fly down into the trout stream. You can also add weight or a beadhead to most patterns. You'll find this works better than adding split shot and putty to your leader or tippet. Heavy and bulky nymph hooks must be able to withstand underwater abuse.

Dry fly hooks are generally thinner and less likely to dive deep and become wedged between rocks or stuck into the side of a log. The lighter weight hooks will also help the fly float on top of the water and stay positioned in a more life like silhouette. Don't be surprised if a big trout sometimes straightens out a dry fly hook.

Most beginning tiers—and anglers—use size 12 hooks. Properly proportioned flies tied on this size of dry and nymph hooks can accurately imitate insects in many areas. Obviously, big stoneflies require larger hooks and Tricos require much smaller hooks. Once you tie a few patterns and become adept at casting and flyfishing, consider moving down to size 14 or 16. I have found the smaller flies and hooks look daintier, are more likely to dance on the water surface

Insect eggs cover the underside of a rock ledge.

when you twitch the tip of your fly rod, and are more likely to be favorably viewed by trout and accepted. Yes, the smaller flies are harder to tie and more difficult to tie onto the tippet, but they work.

When in doubt, consult with a local fly shop or look at Web sites and catalogs to get a general idea about what size hook to use when tying a fly and when fishing a body of water. When in doubt, err on the smaller size. You are trying to mimic natural insects and as trout view a pattern in clear water, the water can magnify the fly and make it look slightly larger.

Reminder: the smaller the number, the larger the hook. A size 24 is a tiny hook. When possible, fish the smallest size hook and fly that you can when using dry flies. The fish seem more willing to eat smaller, natural floating fly imitation.

THE BASIC HOOK SIZES OF FLIES

DRY FLIES

Blue Winged Olive	14-22
Adams	10-24
Ants	16-22
Light Cahill	12-20
Hoppers and Crickets	10-14

NYMPHS

Hare's Ear	10-18
Midges Pupas	16-22

STREAMERS/WORMS

Woolly Worm	8-12
Muddler Minnow	6-12

Tying a fly's head and securing the material to the hook is easily accomplished
with the use of overhand loops that are pulled tight
against the material and hook's shank.

10 | *Tie Your Own Flies*

MUDDLER MINNOW

(Streamer)
Popular Sizes:
02, 04, 06, 08, 10, 12
Hook Type:
4X long streamer
Thread:
Black 6/0
Tail:
Mottled turkey quill segments
Body:
Flat gold tinsel
Wing:
Underwing: gray squirrel tail.
Overwing: mottled turkey quill segments.
Head:
Spun natural gray deer hair, clipped to shape leaving untrimmed natural ends extending toward bend as a collar.

Fly tying can be nearly as addicting as fly-fishing. Tying flies can also reduce stress, help you catch more fish and save you money. If you become good at tying flies you can also make money. Tying can help you stock up and avoid being caught short on fish-favored flies and adds an enhanced level of enjoyment for many anglers.

Flies can be very effective for catching trout, not to mention pan-fish, bass and saltwater fishes. Did I mention that tying flies can also be fun? Tying a fly is a simple matter of twisting materials, feathers and thread onto a bare hook. Anyone can tie flies with a little practice and patience. Once you learn the basics and a few simple knots, you can quickly expand your portfolio of patterns. The most critical skills for any beginner is learning the knots and keeping the fly's parts—tail, body, wings and hackle—in proportion and secure on the hook.

A basic fly can cost more than $2 in most stores. A basic fly tying kit costs about $40. After you tie less than 20 flies, the kit has paid for itself. Money saved can mean more fishing trips and you'll have more flies in your pocket.

Fly Terminology

An artificial fly is constructed by winding one material after another onto a hook. Most flies are built from the tail at the bend of the hook forward to the head, which is normally located at the hook's eye. After you select a pattern, you should secure the required materials and prepare and organize them. This may involve cutting a section from a large feather or pulling a wad of fur from a plastic bag. Much of the preparation depends on the pattern that you plan to tie.

Next, select a hook that works proportionally with the pattern you plan to build. Dry flies—the most popular—use lightweight hooks so the finished fly will stay on the water's surface. Nymphs, wet flies and streamers use heavier hooks to slide underwater and withstand the wear and tear of bumping into rocks and obstructions. Fly types include: attractors, imitators and search patterns. While most fly patterns represent some stage of insect life, flies can also imitate larger fare such as frogs, crayfish and minnows.

Assorted hackles, the feathers from a chicken's neck, are used to tie many fly patterns.

A vice, tying materials and a pattern book are all that are needed to begin wrapping material onto a hook.

and other materials have pushed fly tying into a new realm.

There are thousands of hook styles and sizes but fortunately most patterns provide specific details about which hook works best. When tying, however, take note that the larger the hook's number, the smaller the hook's size. A #24 is nearly microscopic while a #10 is large. Most dry flies are tied on the #12 to #14 size hooks.

History's first report of artificial fishing flies was in ancient Macedonia during the third century A.D. The report said that the natives fastened yellow cock feathers to a hook with red wool. The patterns and materials of flies has been slow to change over the centuries since the habits of old tiers are generally hard to break—until now. Moving ahead, in the 1970s many synthetic materials were introduced into fly tying and the number of fly patterns has since dramatically exploded. In recent years colored markers, plastic wings, new colors, enhanced yarns

If you travel and fish, you can take along a basic tying kit and create a pattern to match local insects that you capture and observe. Flytiers can be a quirky lot, so be forewarned before you go in too deep! Tying flies can also help you custom design flies to meet your local insect population's unique characteristics. Some insect species vary with subtle regional differences. For example, golden stoneflies and black stoneflies in some western areas are large 2-inch-long insects. Stoneflies in the East, however, are about an inch long.

If you decide that fly tying is for you, consider buying a kit complete with a vice, hooks, feathers, fur and a good pattern book. Some fly shops offer these kits as part of their courses, and other shops offer custom kits suitable for regional patterns. If you must cut corners and save costs, forgo the bags and packages of materials and get enough items to tie the top-five patterns. Do not skimp on a vice because a flimsy and flexible vice

will lead to frustration. A vice should be solid because you'll want to apply pressure to the hook and all knots. The tighter that you can make a whip finish or knot on your fly, the longer it will stay together. Flies take a lot of abuse both from sharp fish teeth and when bumped through gravel and rocks when fished subsurface.

The purpose of a tied fly is to attract the attention of a trout and solicit a strike. The fly—a combination of materials wound and lashed to a metal hook—is supposed to accurately mimic a natural insect in color, size and silhouette. Some of the common characteristics common to a fly and its true-to-life insect counterpart are often very easy to identify. The more that you know about the local insects, the easier it will be to select a matching fly.

If you want to tie these patterns on your own, look for the complete kits that some fly shops offer. These mini kits generally have the hooks, materials, thread and a pattern guide in one ready-to-purchase bag. There are also several Web sites and CD-ROM programs that can show you great detail about tying many popular fly patterns. As you advance you should be able to look at a fly and have a basic understanding of how it was constructed and be able to determine some of the materials used in its construction.

You can vary the pattern somewhat

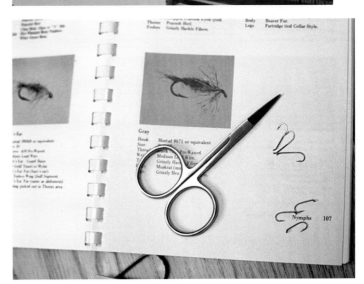

CD-ROMs have joined books as great sources of patterns. Some CDs include videos that teach how to tie a particular fly pattern.

and still create a fly that will catch fish. Some flies, for example, call for a certain hook from a manufacturer (Umpqua, Orvis and Mustad are the big ones) and specific items like rabbit or muskrat fur. You can move up or down the scale in the size hook recommended, substitute other similar hooks and substitute synthetic fur for the more expensive natural fur. As long as you stay reasonably close

Pattern books guide how to tie flies that imitate real-world insects, and fine-point scissors help sculpt natural materials on tiny hooks.

to the intended design the fish often cannot detect the difference. Remember that the fly is being washed in by currents and a trout has a microsecond fraction to determine if it will bite or pass.

As you advance and increase your tying skills, you may decide to compete in a tying contest. These can often be very competitive. You'll often see hand-tied flies at these events that will make the real insect look fake. Newly designed and created materials in recent years—especially opaque wings with veins—have helped tiers everywhere increase the grade of their flies. And as a rule, if you see something that

you like in a fly shop, consider buying one or two for patterns. Most shops know what you are doing, but they also welcome your business.

Flies hold an almost mystical symbolism for some anglers. You'll spot trout fishing flies on ceramic dinnerware, shot glasses, lamps and lampshades, shirts, hats, belts, jackets, business cards and almost anything to decorate the home. A quick glance at a fly often evokes images of remote areas in the great outdoors. There are also businesses that specialize in custom presentation flies. You can obtain flies under a glass dome— looks like it's to prevent it from

This fly tying class at Bentley's Outfitters in Eden Prairie, Minnesota, teaches anglers about tying patterns that are effective in local streams. This is a popular winter activity for many fly anglers and a great way to meet new fishing partners.

flying away—or in matted and framed shadow boxes and picture frames. When you spot these in a home, you know you're among enthusiasts.

Choose a Hook

The size of hook you use to tie a fly will determine how the fly lands and sits on the water, and how a fish sees it. Hooks for nymph and streamer patterns are often thicker and heavier. The additional weight helps pull the fly down into the depths of the trout stream. You can also add weight or a beadhead to most patterns to achieve increased weight. You'll find this works better than adding split shot and putty to your leader or tippet. Heavy and bulky nymph hooks must be able to withstand underwater abuse.

Dry fly hooks are generally thinner and less likely to dive deep and become wedged between rocks or stuck into the side of a log. The lighter weight hooks will also help the fly float on top of the water and stay positioned in a more life like silhouette. Don't be surprised if a big trout sometimes straightens out a dry fly hook.

Most beginning tiers—and anglers—use size 12 hooks. Properly proportioned flies tied on this size dry and nymph hooks can accurately imitate many insects in many areas. Obviously, big stone-flies require larger hooks and Tricos require much smaller hooks. Once you tie a few patterns and become adept at casting and flyfishing, consider moving down to size 14 or 16. I have found the smaller flies and hooks look more dainty, are more likely to dance on the water surface when you twitch the tip of your fly rod, and are more likely to be favorably viewed by trout and accepted. Yes, the smaller flies are harder to tie and more difficult to tie onto the tippet, but they work.

When in doubt, consult with a local fly shop or look at Web sites and catalogs to get a general idea about what size hook to use when tying a fly and when fishing a body of water. When in doubt, err on the smaller size. You are trying to mimic natural insects and as trout view a pattern in clear water, the water will magnify the fly and make it look slightly larger.

TIP:

A unique and special Christmas gift that you can create for family and friends is a hand-tied fly placed inside a clear glass Christmas ornament. Royal Coachman streamers and dry flies look the best dressed for the season. As you are tying the fly, secure fine tippet material to the center of the fly, and then secure this to the clip used for hanging the ornament. The fly will look as if it's flying around inside the glass bulb in a natural position.

PARTS OF A FLY

Most trout flies have standard parts. These include the: tail, body, wing, hackle and head. If the pattern calls for a weighted body, you'll have to secure the weight material to the hook's shank before beginning construction of the fly. Most beginners wrap too much material onto the fly and create a big, thick body and fluffy fly. Remember that most insects are small, thin and frail, like the dainty mayfly. It is always better to apply material on the conservative side. The less material that you tie on, the lighter the total weight and the more naturally the fly will ride on the water surface. Some nymphs, streamers and wet flies can have big and elaborate bodies that must be constructed in layers or segments.

FLY FAVORITES

For beginners and advanced anglers alike, the question arises: Which fly should I use, or which flies should I pack along for the fishing trip? The top-five all-around flies, according to experts and some of my friends who fish for a living, include the Adams, with its classic upright wings, the Blue Winged Olive, Gold-Ribbed Hare's Ear (beadhead version when possible), the Prince nymph, and the Elk Hare Caddis. These and other popular flies are shown below and on the following page.

NYMPHS

THE FLY FORMERLY KNOWN
AS PRINCE

GOLD-RIBBED HARE'S EAR

BEADHEAD PHEASANT TAIL

BEADHEAD EMERGING
SPARKLE CADDIS

BRASSIE

KAUFMANN'S STONE

FLASHBACK SCUD

WET FLIES

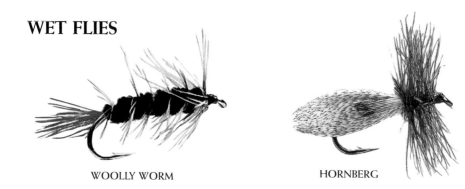

WOOLLY WORM

HORNBERG

DRY FLIES

ADAMS

ROYAL COACHMAN

BLUE WINGED OLIVE

ROYAL WULFF

CDC ELK WING CADDIS

DAVE'S HOPPER

HARD BODY ANT

TRAVIS PARA MIDGE

STREAMERS

MUDDLER MINNOW

WOOLLY BUGGER

BLACK NOSE DACE

TYING A NYMPH

Starting the thread on a hook for a beadhead nymph pattern.

Wrapping the body material on the hook.

A completed beadhead Prince's nymph with peacock hearl body and brass bead, along with goose wing biots outer wings.

Lighted magnifying glasses can be a great aid when tying tiny nearly microscopic flies.

A Good Start

For a beginner, the woolly worm pattern—a caterpillar-like fly—is hard to beat as a first pattern. The standard hook sizes for this pattern are #6 to #10. A woolly worm uses a large, heavy wire hook that provides more weight to help the fly sink underwater. Standard woolly worm body colors include: yellow, black, brown and olive.

Before you begin twisting your thread around a hook, take the time to select a well-lighted and quiet tying area. This process requires concentration and you need to be able to see small materials well. Make sure that the area—such as a tabletop—has ample workspace and that there are no breezes to move fine, light-weight materials. Feathers and other lightweight materials used to create flies can move on the slightest breeze and you'll become frustrated when you have to chase down a feather or corner a section of yarn instead of tying them to the hook.

Next, lay out all necessary tools and the required materials for the fly you wish to build. The more organized that you are, the easier this process goes. Some tiers prepare the material for a dozen flies at one time and then tie each complete fly before starting the next one. This works well for me and I find that my technique improves with each fly that I tie. Sometimes I toss out the first one or cut the hook out and start over. Other tiers like to tie on a dozen tails, then tie on a dozen bodies and work their way through this process until they have a dozen completed flies. You'll have to determine which method works best for you.

The second most important material after the selection of the hook is the thread. Black, pre-waxed, nylon, size 6/0 works well for most applications. Applying the thread with a bobbin will help you better manage the thread. If you do not have a bobbin, cut about 12 to 20 inches of thread to complete most fly patterns. If you come up short, you can tie in new thread and continue building the fly.

The woolly worm pattern uses chenille or yarn for its body and a small piece of red yarn or feather for the tail. Some anglers believe that fish are attracted to red. The woolly worm also uses a single brown or grizzly feather—or hackle—wrapped around the fly's body. The feather should match the hook size and not appear too bushy. The barbs—individual strands—of the feather will simulate insect legs and make the fly appear to crawl to a hungry trout.

TYING A DRY FLY

After securing the thread to the dry fly hook, tie on the tail.

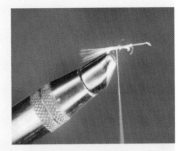

Wrap a body from rear to front and make an enlarged thorax as you keep components into natural proportions.

Tying on a pair of dry fly wings.

The completed dry fly with the hackle wrapped around the wings. The hackle appears to underwater fish as insect legs, and aids the angler in being able to spot the fly on the water and observe if a trout possibly takes it.

TYING A DRY FLY: WOOLLY WORM continued on page 124

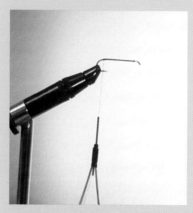

Place the hook in the vice and secure the vice jaws at the hook's bend with enough pressure to securely hold the hook in place.

A bobin will help you control the tying thread and apply pressure as you construct the fly.

A piece of red yarn is tied into place to build the tail of this woolly worm fly. The excess material is cut away.

Begin Building

Most patterns are tied from the bend of the hook forward to the eye. After you select a single hook, place it in the vice—normally with the edge of the tip of the vice's jaws holding the hook by the bottom of its bend—and tighten the vice's jaws. Apply enough grip force to keep the hook from moving when moderate pressure is applied on the hook's eye. Normally the tip of the hook protrudes slightly from the tip of the vice jaws. Next, you'll wrap the thread over the hook's shank—from the bend forward to just behind the eye, and back—and tie it off with a couple of overhand loops. You'll find that it is easier to use one continuous piece of thread so be careful to not cut the thread until the fly is finished and the final head wrap is in place. Remember to keep all materials tight and uniform during the construction process.

THE STEPS

Tie on a section of red yarn or feather for the tail with an approximately ½-inch length of yarn extending behind the bend of the hook. Use approximately six tight wraps of thread to hold the tail in place and then tie an overhand loop over the wraps. A bobbin will help you place the wraps on top of each other and keep them tight. Trim off any excess yarn that is over the hook's shank and be careful to not cut the thread from the bobbin.

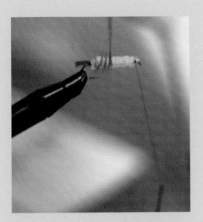

The body material is tied into place at the hook's bend. The tying thread is wrapped forward around the shank up to the eye and secured in place.

Hackle pliers help manage feathers and keep wraps uniform when building a fly.

Use hackle pliers to wrap a palmered feather around the woolly worm's body material. The feather will simulate legs.

If you find that the tail, or any material, shifts as you are tying, try placing the material on the side of the hook. It will normally ride up and into place as you tighten the thread. Experiment to determine what works for you.

STEP 1

Tie on a palmered or fuzzed hackle with wraps of thread and secure in place with an overhand loop. Running your fingertips down the feather from tip to base will cause the feather barbs to protrude outward. The tip of the feather should point back and away from the vice as you tie it onto the hook, then you pull it over and wrap forward as you begin to build the fly.

STEP 2

Tie on the yellow chenille or yarn for the body and secure in place.

STEP 3

Wrap the tying thread forward over the hook's shank and secure it behind the hook's eye with overhand loops, then tightly twist the chenille around the hook's shank forward to the eye. Leave about $\frac{1}{16}$-inch of open space behind the hook's eye to tie the head. Be sure to wrap the body material evenly and in tight circles so that it covers the shank and builds up a body about one-half the diameter of a pencil.

STEP 4

Secure the body material behind the eye with tying thread. Check to be certain the material is tight and does not move when pressure is applied.

TYING A DRY FLY: WOOLLY WORM continued from page 123

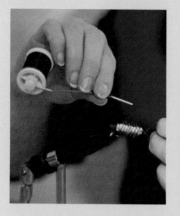 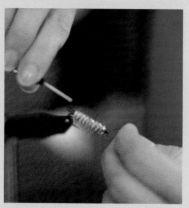 

Tying a fly's head and securing the material to the hook is easily accomplished with the use of overhand loops that are pulled tight against the material and hook's shank. The loop or half-hitch can be made by wrapping the tying thread around two fingers and then looping it back across the hook.

A small drop of tier's cement will help keep the thread wraps that form the fly's head in place and keep material from being untied by a fish's sharp teeth.

STEP 5

Wrap the hackle forward over the body material with evenly spaced wraps to give the fly a segmented appearance. Hackle pliers will help you control the feather and apply pressure. Secure the hackle behind the eye with the tying thread.

STEP 6

Make a finishing knot to build up a slight head behind the eye. Remember to keep all parts of the fly in proportion to the hook and overall fly size. A finishing knot is an overhand loop with multiple loops of the thread upon previous loops. This is the stage where most beginning tiers get into trouble. They tie too close to the eye and then wrap thread over the eye and have little or no space to pass the tippet through the eye. If you are crowding the eye, pinch the fly body at the front and slightly slide it back on the hook shank to increase the room that you have to tie the head.

STEP 7

Apply a coat of tier's cement to bond the thread into place and to give the fly a solid insect-like head appearance. You might have to re-open the hook's eye with a needle after the cement dries.

After you tie a few flies, you'll be able to look at any fly and understand how it's constructed. Any well-stocked fly shop should have the materials you'll need to tie any fly. Some shops stock fly pattern kits that include all the hooks and mate-

The trout fly does a good job of mimicking Mother Nature.

rials needed to tie a dozen flies of one pattern, and some shops give discounts if you purchase a new vice and their preassembled beginner's kit. Other shops offer in-store classes and include the price of a vice and basic tying materials in the class tuition or offer them at a greatly reduced price. There are also several Web sites that exhibit fly patterns and some that sell tying materials. Two possible sources—www. cabelas.com and www.orvis.com— sometimes have articles about tying flies and information about new fly tying materials.

In addition to the cost savings and education you'll gain from tying your own flies, the best thrill is seeing a rising trout—or any fish— make a wild dash for your fly and then explode through the water's surface as it realizes it's hooked.

You'll be hooked too!

Most fly bodies are narrow at the tail end and then bulk slightly before tapering again near the eye. From underwater, fish see a dark object on the water's surface and focus on the shape more often than the color. For underwater flies, color becomes important because the fish can observe the light spectrums reflected by the fly's material.

When tying the upright wings on a dry fly, remember that most wings are small, even sized and stand upright. A wrap of thread at the base, and wrapping hackle tightly in front and behind, the wings will help keep them in their proper position.

Patience is a trademark of good fly-tiers.

ROYAL COACHMAN

(Dry Fly)
Popular Sizes:
12, 14, 16
Hook Type:
Extra-fine dry fly
Thread:
Black 6/0
Tail:
Golden pheasant tippets or brown hackle fibers.
Body:
Peacock herl in two sections with a red floss center band.
Wing:
White duck wing quill segments—upright and divided.
Hackle:
Brown

When flyfishing from a float tube, wear a personal floatation device (PFD) to be safe. The author's wife, Reuth (below), is fishing in western North Carolina.

11 | *Float-Tubing for Fishing Fun*

ROYAL WULFF

(Dry Fly)
Popular Sizes:
10, 12, 14, 16, 18
Hook Type:
Extra-fine dry fly
Thread:
Black 6/o
Tail:
Brown bucktail (for larger sizes) or natural elk or deer hair.
Body:
In three sections: front and rear third of peacock herl, middle third of red floss or substitute.
Wing:
White calf tail (white calf body hair for the smaller sizes)—upright and divided.
Hackle:
Brown, hackled heavily

Float tubes can help you reach areas—and sometimes big fish—that other anglers cannot touch. The popularity of float tubes is skyrocketing as anglers discover the advantages offered by these small inflatable wonders. First and foremost, the highly portable, donut- or horseshoe-shaped personal rafts can boldly go where aluminum or drift boats often can't because of shallow waters or restricted access points with narrow trails. This includes small lakes, ponds, mountain trout lakes and other bodies of water that are devoid of ramps or where vehicle access is restricted by law.

Float tube options have increased along with the demand for float tubes. Today's buyer can be overwhelmed by the many styles, colors and options. Cabela's offers nearly a dozen models and there are numerous other manufacturers. When shopping, remember that you will find models that can also be used for hunting so that you can easily stretch your recreation dollars.

While the most popular use for these tubes continues to be fly fishermen after trout, more and more freshwater anglers are using them to pursue all types of fish in nearly all types of waters. Float tubes can place you at the center of the action with minimal fuss.

No Kicking Tires Here

When buying a float tube there are important construction details to take into account. One design factor to consider when trying out a float tube is to determine if you can easily enter and exit the model that you're interested in. Some tubes are too small inside for large-framed anglers. You'll also want to look closely for double-stitched seams, reinforced stress points, sturdy straps, and an exterior shell construction using a durable fabric such as DuPont's Cordura. Choose a tube with lots of pockets to store small tackle boxes, lunch and other fly-fishing gear. For increased comfort, select a model with a high back and a wide panel seat. Some better-designed models make you feel like you are sitting in a recliner in your den and make each fishing trip a true relaxing pleasure. Avoid any model that has you suspended

Flyfishing in a mountain lake from a float tube.

You'll want to put your fins on while in the water since it is nearly impossible to walk on land while wearing them.

solely on straps because these can reduce blood circulation in your legs and will soon make you uncomfortable and cold. If you select a horseshoe type float tube, be certain the model has a strong spreader bar in the front to brace the ends apart. Examine several models and choose one that you will enjoy for years to come because float tubes will last that long if properly cared for and when kept out of deteriorating sunlight.

Another must-have tube accessory

for anglers is an on-board rod holder—a Velcro wrap pad. No one wants to see a $600 fly rod disappear like a diving submarine. You can also help avoid this with a rod leash—a simple string and loop that attaches to the end of your fly rod. D-rings are also much welcome accessories for securing gear to your float tube. If you have more gear, look into possibly using straps to secure the load. Bulky gear like a raincoat can be lashed to the back of many float tube models where it's out of the way while you're casting.

Float tubes are typically propelled by a pair of fins that are lashed or strapped to your boots. Some fins float and some fins sink. If the fins you have are not buoyant, you can secure them to your footwear with a short piece of cord. A word of caution about putting on fins and heading straight for the water—you probably won't make it without falling. When you put fins on, normal walking becomes nearly impossible. You'll need to walk backwards or slowly side-step to reach the water. I recommend always wearing wading boots or sturdy footwear while float-tubing since rocks, stumps, and broken glass can lurk in any water. Take a wrong step on these obstacles and your trip will quickly end.

You'll find that moving backwards in a float tube is easy. You simply kick with your legs extended in front of you, and this motion propels you backwards. When you reach the area where you want to cast, just kick with one leg and the tube will spin around and place you facing in the right direction. If you'd like to stay in one location and fish an extended period of time, consider purchasing a float tube anchor.

Okay, for those of you who want to save your energy for casting and winching in big trout, you might want to consider purchasing a motor. You can purchase a mini tube with a platform that accepts any battery and a trolling motor. Using these does take some coordination and experimentation to get the process right.

One question that faces all float-tubers is whether or not to wear waders. I always do when fishing in cold trout waters. Tubing without waders, however, is a good way to cool off on a hot summer day. Remember also that the longer you stay in frigid trout waters, the colder your core body temperature becomes. You'll want to avoid hypothermia and be flexible and mobile enough to return to shore.

And as a precautionary note, remember to always wear a U.S. Coast Guard approved PFD—per-

QUICK, OUT OF THE WATER!

Okay, for those anglers who don't want to be down in a tube and bobbing along, many manufacturers now offer alternatives—pontoon boats. I quickly spotted 10 models in one flyfishing equipment catalog. These small boat-like craft have two independent inflatable pods to place you higher over the water surface for increased visibility. They can be rowed and maneuvered through smaller rapids, and normally have very comfortable seats. There's also room on board for lots of accessories and you can anchor a pontoon boat into strategic locations as you flyfish. Some models are easily broken down and packed after the trip.

Most models cost considerably more than a simple float tube. The prices range from $300 to $500 for most one-man pontoon boats—two-man models cost more. Take note that most pontoon models are powered by oars, but some models accept a battery and trolling motor. Learning to row and maneuver the boat on a steadily flowing river requires great effort for some anglers. Others prefer to anchor the pontoon while they wade into the best fishing areas to stand as they cast. If you take the easy route and use a motor to propel your pontoon boat, check the local boating regulations to see if you'll need state motorboat registration numbers. This varies from state to state.

sonal flotation device. The new USCG approved inflatable suspenders, or Sospenders, can increase your chances of reaching land if something goes wrong. Another option is a PFD vest that's designed as a fishing vest with exterior pockets. For cold, early-spring days, or for float-tubing when ice and snow are around, consider wearing a floatation coat. Yes, these floating overcoats can be expensive, but the newer styles are more wearer-friendly and you can move freely to cast. If you are going into waters with motorboats around, you might also possibly use a flag on a pole to reveal your presence. After you've geared up, it's time to take the plunge.

Many rafting companies also will take fly fisherman down a river, and some companies only take anglers. Lake rubber rafts are very popular in the Western states and in parts of West Virginia.

On the Water Action

Before you fin away, consider properly securing and storing things you don't want to lose, including all valuables. I bring a limited amount of flies, fly boxes and other items with me while using a float tube. I carefully select my flies or lures and place those in small clear-plastic tackle boxes that are then zipped up inside of the tube's pockets. I increase my fishing time by reducing the time spent searching through storage containers looking for the right item. If your fly box has a loop or ring on it, secure the box to the float tube with a small section of strong string. Some fly boxes arrive pre-rigged just for this purpose.

When you are changing flies, try to work over the front netting or apron in the tube. If you should drop an item, this surface should catch it for you.

Tricks for Tubers

There are several things you can do to make float tube trips easier. When possible, drift along with the wind or water movement. If a breeze is blowing where you are fishing, or if there is a slight current, let the wind and water do the work for you. You'll drift along like a mayfly with the right wind at your back.

You should obviously avoid waterfalls and white-capped water when using a float tube. Follow the manufacturer's recommendations and consider your personal skill level before plunging into rough water and white-capped lakes. A strong wind could push you away from shore and cause a grave situation. If the water is so rough that you have to struggle to stay alive, you'll have little time to fish.

When flyfishing, you might find that one of the newer 10- or 11-foot fly rods will help you gain more reach with each cast and keep flies overhead instead of perilously close to your ears. You also might need the longer reach provided by these lengthy rods to keep flies and hooks well away from the tube. Always wear a hat and sunglasses to keep stray hooks from snagging you in vital areas. And take note that anyone in a float tube becomes a mini island for bugs. You'll want to pack some bug spray or a mesh suit, such as a Bug-Out Outdoorwear jacket, on board.

Float tubes are more than a poor man's boat. I like the facts that they are quiet, portable, inexpensive and relaxing. You can slip in on feeding fish and sometimes catch fish after fish without changing locations. My wife and I have used ours while traveling across the United States and pack them, the PFDs, and the fins into a duffel bag along with other fishing gear and vests. We deflate them at home, then re-inflate them by the water with a small pump that plugs into the car's cigarette lighter. This system is very convenient when flying or when storage space is at a premium in your car.

I see more and more float tubes riding the surface on waters everywhere. From the smiles on the users' faces, I know that they've discovered the secrets of float-tubing.

FLOAT-TUBING GEAR CONTACTS:

Bug-Out Outdoorwear clothing/ www.bug-out-outdoorwear.com/ 641-437-4805

Boatman Pontoons/ 801-479-3451

Buck's Bags for float tubes and pontoons/ 800-284-2247

Cabela's gear and float tubes/ www.cabelas.com/ 800-237-4444

Caddis—one of the oldest names in float tubes/ 800-422-3347

Fly Tech for float tubes/ 800-590-2281

J.W. Outfitters—pontoon boats/ 619-471-2171

Predator—large capacity float tubes/ 603-749-0526

The Creek—open-faced float tubes/ 800-843-8454

*Standing off to the side and drifting a fly over likely areas is the
only way to fish some smaller waters.*

12 *Where the Fish Are*

THE FLY FORMERLY KNOWN AS PRINCE

(Nymph)
Popular Sizes:
12, 14, 16, 18
Hook Type:
Traditional 2X long nymph hook
Thread:
Red 8/o
Tail:
Two brown goose biots, slayed using ball of red thread.
Body:
2-4 fibers of peacock herl.
Ribbing:
Flat gold tinsel
Wing:
Two pieces of holographic film cut in the shape of biots.
Hackle:
Brown rooster

Knowing where the fish are is an important first step to catching them. While almost every river in the United States has unique characteristics, they also share many similarities. Most waters will have pools, riffles, sand bars, eddies, boulders, root-wads and other habitat to contend with. The vegetation on the bank—and its proximity to the water's edge—is the greatest variable in most trout waters. Once you know what to look for, you can normally determine where the trout are and how to place your fly to gain their attention and favor.

One of the worst things a fly angler can do on any water at any destination is rig up quickly and dash to the water. I see this all the time. Fly-fishing should be fun and relaxing, not a competition. The valuable time you spend observing water, looking for insects and watching for feeding fish, can greatly multiply your catch rate. It helps to have a goal when you set out. Mine is often to simply have a good time and to catch one fish. Anything else is a bonus. If you must catch a trout as long as your arm and bigger than you have ever caught before, then you are setting yourself up for fail-

ure. If you are driven to catch more fish than your partner, fish more water distance or make more casts to impress someone or prove a point, maybe you should find someone else to fish with or switch to another species. Trout fishing should be fun—period.

Trout key in one habitat and you should seek this out. Just as you prefer types of cars, styles of homes and colors of furniture and clothes, trout have preferences. They seek a place that will provide overhead shelter—or where shelter is close by—and a place where they can find food. The spot must also have water that delivers oxygen, is at a comfortable temperature and has the right amount of flow to keep the fish in place without washing it away. If remaining in a location requires more energy from a trout than it gains from remaining in that place, the fish must move or perish.

Safety

There are numerous places in many rivers for a trout to find safety. Large structures that cast dark shadows and prevent direct overhead

An angler casts a fly into the water above a riffle. Trout normally hang in riffles facing upstream to wait for food.

bank to provide a safe haven for trout. In most states these expensive stream enhancement projects have been funded through the sale of special trout stamps and licenses.

Fish readily take to these structures if they are properly built and installed. At one site in Wisconsin a fisheries biologist saw a huge trout move into a new subsurface shelf structure while a crew was still working with a backhoe to place fill on top of the structure. In some cases the larger fish rules the water and has first choice on the best sites, as was the case with the new fish shelf. After hearing the biologist's report about the structures, I went there myself to explore and observe. After seeing a huge trout dash out to grab a high-drifting mayfly, I cast my imitation. The big brown graced me with a strike.

There are other places to focus your search for trout. Deep pools often have numerous eroded side pockets that can become havens for trout. The fish stay in the less violent water along the sides or at the bottom and avoid detection because of the depth, white waterfall spill, or dark green colors found in most deep pools. The rushing water pushes food down deep to the trout.

Another popular trout shelter is among stream vegetation. From beds of moss and watercress to islands of weeds, fish like to hide among nearly undetectable channels in these spots. Don't overlook

views are usually preferred. This keeps birds from diving in and grabbing the fish. Shade also reduces glare on the water's surface and helps fish see items on the surface that they might wish to eat.

Many structures provide safe havens for trout. Among them are logs, root-wads, large boulders, undercut banks, and overhanging weeds and trees. Numerous streams now have man-made shelves or wooden cribs implanted under the these in your search for a place to cast. Casting can be difficult in and around weed beds but the effort can yield big results.

Food

Fish, while they are not lazy, like to have food come to them. Water acts like a food conveyor belt and it moves dislodged nymphs, injured minnows, and any unlucky beetle, bee, or earthworm that plunges into the water and hence into the feeding lane of a waiting fish. Fish lie in wait and will move up and slightly left or right in an effort to capture food. A trout will not swim across a wide river to take your fly or grab a dainty mayfly. First, it might not see the insect or your fly, and second, the

longer a fish is exposed to overhead dangers, the less chance it has to survive. Life in a trout stream is a constant struggle of survival. It's a world of eat and possible be eaten.

In this riffle in the obscured water would be a good place to cast your fly.

Water Hydraulics

The speed of a current varies greatly across a stream and at various depths. Along the edges and bottom of a stream or river where the moving water encounters obstacles,

In and along this line of riffling water would be a place to seek trout.

This angler has located a deep pool below rushing water—the possible home of a large trout.

Deadfalls and submerged logs are a great place to find a trout.

Water around man-made structures, like fences and log cribs, can hold trout.

it is slower flowing. The obstacles act much like friction brakes against the water.

On the surface and along the edge of the slower water zones, the water moves down a river at a medium speed. Fish will readily move into this zone to feed without expending too much energy.

For a channelized river, the core of the water passing through the valley is the fastest rushing water. This water is unencumbered and the valley could be considered to be like a huge tunnel or pipe with water gushing through it. Fish will avoid this water when possible because they can be swept downstream or must use a lot of energy to stay in their territory. The exact location of this rushing water channel varies greatly. A sharp bend in the river, a huge midstream boulder, and other obstacles can change or divert this swift water. Take your time and read the water to determine what is happening before you.

Adjusting the depth of your fly by a few inches can often drop it out, or raise it above the rushing water zone, and make it more acceptable to a hungry fish. When in doubt, experiment and observe to fish effectively.

Eddies

While trout generally lie and face upstream, this is not always the case. A large boulder or a sand bar at the end of a pool can cause an eddy—a situation where the water spins in a circular motion. If conditions are right, such as a thick layer of top water foam or an undercut bank along the edge of an eddy, a fish might lie in there. It's sheltered overhead from danger, and the food is washing to it. In some cases this means the fish is facing downstream. If you see a fish feeding in an eddy, try to determine which way the fish is rising and subsequently dropping. If it is moving toward the back of the pool and actually facing downstream, you'll need to adjust your cast to let the fly fall short and be washed back upstream and through the fish's feeding lane.

Eddies can also form on the upstream and downstream side of

boulders. Eddies will also form at sharp bends, around islands and at obstacles like the end of logs and tree roots. This is where you will be greatly rewarded if you slow down and try to determine which direction the water is traveling in an eddy. Small leaves, pieces of debris and other floating materials will often reveal which direction the water is moving. This can in turn give clues about where the fish are. Wearing polarized sunglasses can help you cut through the glare and see into the water to observe debris and fish.

Riffles

Trout love to hang out in riffles—areas where the water is moving along in small gentle waves about 6- to 10 inches tall as it washes over small boulders. Behind each of these boulders is a pocket of calm water caused by the hydraulics of the streamflow. It's hard for a bird to see into the almost white-capped water and a trout can live comfortably there without having to wander or move about in search of food.

Riffles often have underwater changes that you can spot with a calm V that points up- or downstream. An underwater seam is created along the edges of

these Vs. These seams cause foods to move faster or slower, depending upon which side the food is on, and trout use this to their feeding advantage. If you cast and do not get a strike after several attempts on one side of the V, cast and let your fly pass on the other side.

Ebb and Flow

The water patterns you see on the surface of a stream only reveal part of what's happening in the subsurface world. Small swirls can reveal the presence of an underwater rock—a possible fish hiding place—as well as other bottom obstacles and imperfections. Water moves into areas of least resistance—it's a law of physics.

One way to determine how fast water is moving is to toss in a handful of vegetation and observe its travel rate. You can also toss in a fly, or weighted nymph and watch it pass by down deep if the water is clear enough.

TRAVIS PARA MIDGE

(Dry Fly)
Popular Sizes:
16, 18, 20, 22
Additional Colors:
Olive/black, black, gray
Hook Type:
Short-shank curved nymph
Thread:
Black 8/0
Wing:
Olive easy Dubbing
Hackle:
Black or grizzly, parachute style
Abdomen:
Section of microchenille tied over bend of hook and singed at the end.
Thorax:
Fur dubbing

Small watercraft permit anglers to reach spots that are inaccessible from the banks.

Waterfalls create natural fish barriers and migratory trout can often be found in the pool at the bottom of the falls.

TIP:

The best places to concentrate your efforts are at the head of pools and in the riffles. These places often move food, have oxygen and provide cover for trout.

The deep water found in bends in large rivers offers prime habitat where trout can hide from birds and watch for food.

Another way to judge water flow is to wade in. Be cautious and don't get in over your head or into water so powerful that you are swept away. Wading can reveal just how forceful and rapidly moving a river or sections and channels are. Water can be a powerful force. Observe it and respect it.

What Type of Water Is It?

There are two basic mineral loads in trout streams—limestone and freestone. Limestone streams are characterized by high levels of minerals, especially calcium carbonate, and by abundant aquatic vegetation. These streams have insects—midges to mayflies—and crustaceans—scuds to crayfish—on a year-round basis. With lots of food, there can be lots of trout. These streams are often fed by large springs or limited runoff. Some spring fed streams are famous for having huge trout and large fish populations because of near constant year-round temperatures, lush in-stream vegetation and plenty of natural fish foods. Some of these streams in Montana and other states can be fished by permit only because the demand is so great. In some states the fish departments have begun placing blocks of natural minerals into the headwaters of some waterways to increase the mineral content, vegetation and the total fish population. These projects are offering promising results.

Freestone streams frequently originate from melting snows and rain runoff. The current is often swift and the channels deep because the terrain slopes steeply downward.

Freestone streams have low mineral content, sparse vegetation and are subject to violent spring floods. Water levels can plummet dramatically during summer droughts and trout foods can become scarce. Fish populations can be low or widely scattered.

Improving the Waters

Luckily for trout and fly anglers everywhere, many conservation groups and local sportsmen's clubs are working to improve water quality and trout habitat in many waterways.

Erosion places silt into streams and this fine silt can fill pools, raise water temperatures and decrease oxygen levels. In some areas anglers volunteer to plant trees along streams and rivers to reduce erosion and provide the shade that keeps the water cooler and more in line with desired fish temperatures. Fencing is also being used in some areas to keep cattle out of waterways. Manure and highly eroded cattle paths can rapidly degrade a small stream.

In other waterways fly-fishing enthusiasts are working to place structures into the water, such as subsurface shelves, to improve habitat. You can often spot a series of logs anchored to banks with cables in some small streams to create plunge pools and increase dissolved oxygen in the water. These projects often have to be joint efforts between anglers and state or federal conservation departments since federal laws prevent the placement of structures or digging with equipment in many waters. The same holds true for highway projects where roads are moved and trout streams are unnaturally channeled into straight ditches.

In other areas anglers are combining forces to pick up streamside litter and buy or lease right-of-ways. These projects can do wonders to open waterways for fishing and improve the relationship between fly anglers and local landowners. Seek the facts and become an informed and active angler to protect trout habitat. Get involved.

TIP:

If you see a section of water with many mini ripples, this is a stretch of riffles. Fish lie here and can be found ahead of and behind rocks. Just downstream of riffles you will often encounter runs where the water becomes smooth and often deeper.

This deep, shaded pool along a stream bank can conceal lurking trout.

The deep, cool, nutrient-rich tail-water of hydroelectric dams offers an excellent environment for some trout species.

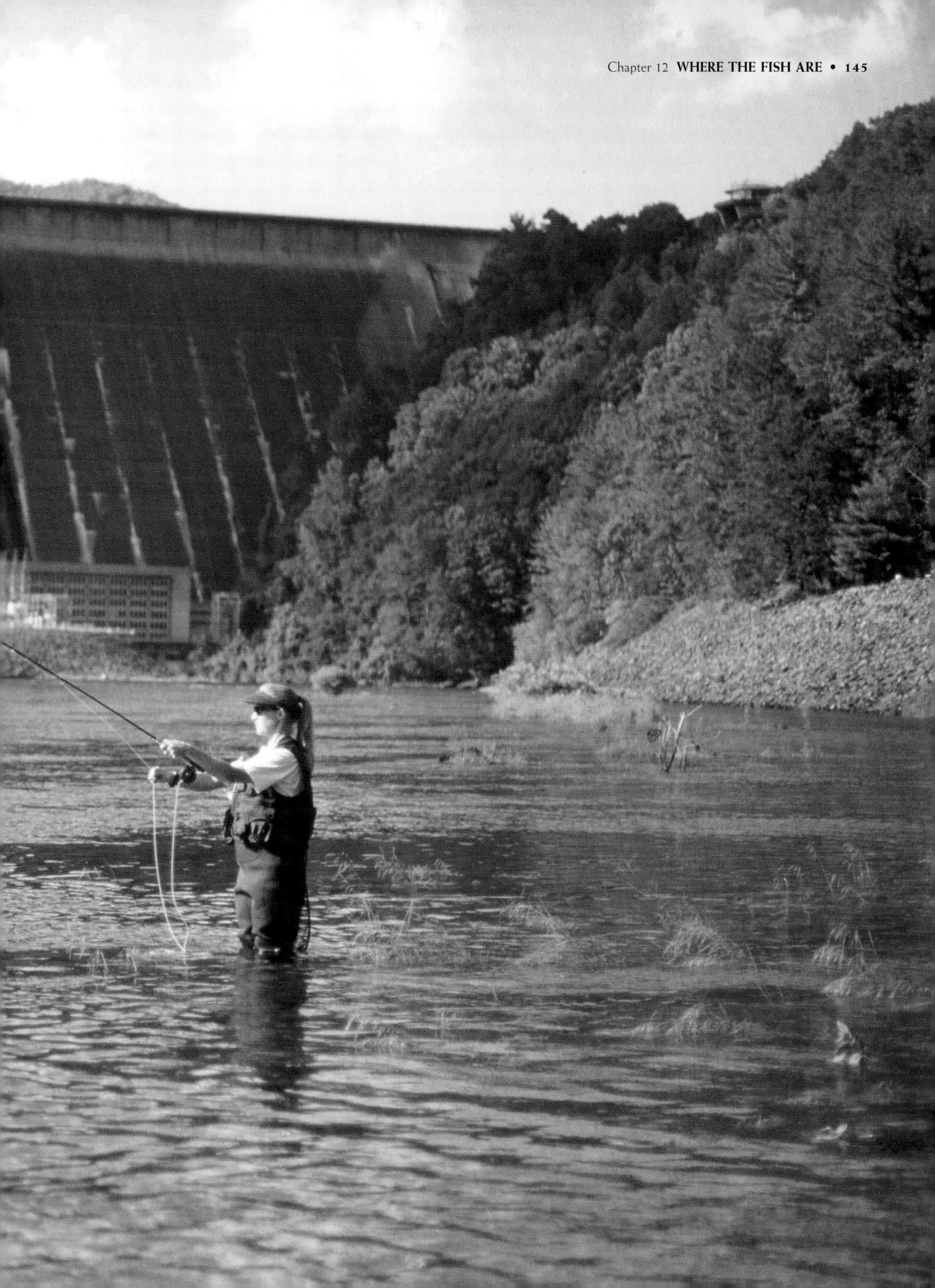

Pick a spot where you suspect a trout will be hiding, such as this seam
where rushing water meets calmer water.

13 | Flyfishing Tactics That Work

Once you have assembled your gear, picked a destination, and walked the stream banks to scout the waters for trout and their habitat, there's only one thing left to do—rig up and let your fly take the deep plunge or high drift.

There are two courses of action for you to pursue: top water and subsurface. Dry flies, foam ants, crickets and grasshoppers rule the topwater world. Nymphs, streamers, wet flies, scud imitations and others help search for trout down in their watery world.

Scouting a River

As you walk the streamside, look for rising fish, insects, feeding birds, other anglers, and the flash of a fish that's fleeing your shadow. Also look for structure that a fish would like to live near. Search for small pools, riffles, pockets of water, natural or man-made barriers and other structures that can scream "fish here!" This is valuable time spent and an investment that can pay big rewards. Why waste time fishing an entire river when sections, and specific areas, offer the best opportunity for your time allotment.

I like to walk away from easy access points and along the stream until the trail grows thin, the brush grows dense and the holes look wilder. Escaping crowds and finding wild fish excite me. Maybe they will excite you too.

The Basics Come Together

Once you have rigged up and are standing streamside, there are a couple of things that you can do to make that first cast a success. First, look up- and downstream for obstacles that could snag your fly or line. Most fly casters fail to take note of what's behind them. This is important information. You need enough distance ahead and behind you to successfully complete a cast. Your line needs to completely unroll upon casting to tug the rod tip with its weight and make your rod load up and effectively move the line.

Next, pick a spot where you suspect—or spotted while scouting—that a fish is hiding. Try to deter-

WOOLLY BUGGER

(Streamer)
Popular Sizes:
04, 06, 08, 10, 12, 14
Additional Colors:
Black, tan, white, olive
Hook Type:
4X long nymph/streamer
Thread:
Black or white 6/0
Tail:
Marabou to match pattern description.
Body:
Chenille to match pattern color.
Ribbing:
Grizzly hackle palmered through body; or hackle color to match pattern color.

Wade along a stream to search for fish, insects and other clues.

mine what's underneath—logs, rocks, weeds, etc., and how deep the obstacles and the fish are. When you cast to or just slightly ahead of this area, you want to prevent hang-ups with your fly. You should be positioned downstream and slightly to one side of the area where you intend to drop your fly.

Most anglers face and fish upstream against the current. You'll find that it's easier to wade this way, you can observe and read the water better, and in most cases you are sneaking in behind a fish that typically lies facing upstream. After you become proficient at fly-fishing and can cast long distances, you will sometimes find it advantageous to fish a large river downstream. This is not the norm and any rocks and sand that you kick loose will alert the trout. If you must fish downstream, wade cautiously and step with finesse.

To begin casting and flyfishing, you'll want to hold the rod in your right hand—if you are right-handed—and pull line from the reel with your left hand. Pull the fly and trailing tippet and leader down the length of the rod and grasp it between the fingers on your casting

hand. You should pull out enough line to create a belly in the fly line and clear any knots and leader and fly line connections from the series of eyes on the rod. Pull more fly line out with your left hand and let the line drop in coils onto the ground or into the water in front of you. Release the fly from your casting hand, and let the leader and your fly swing free. Begin casting by moving the rod back and forth over your right shoulder with the tip slightly out beside your body in a plane. If the line is dropping into the water in front or behind you, you are letting the tip of the rod fall too low or you might not be pushing the rod fast enough. Remember that good casts and tight loops are the result of speeding up your arm movement and bringing the rod tip to an abrupt halt that results in loading the rod. Let the rod spring the fly line into action. That's why you paid all that money for it, now make it work for you.

Don't get frustrated if things are not going your way and you think that your casts are failing. The number one problem for most casters is rushing the rod and not permitting the fly line to completely unfurl. If you hear a crack like a whip, it's the line hitting line in passing and you're not letting the line unfold to roll the tippet and fly out to their full length. Releasing and casting more line can also help load the rod and cause you to slow down. You can look over your shoulder to watch your line unfold behind you and to see how far it reaches.

On Top

Dry flies ride the waves on top of the water because they are light-weight. No need to add weight here because your fly line, leader and tip-pet will carry the super-lightweight fly through the air and gently place it on the water surface. After you securely tie a dry fly to the tippet, you should coat the fly with floatant. If you do not like to have this goop on your fingertips, consider trying spray or dip floatants. After these are applied, the fly should air-dry overnight. If a fly becomes too wet, it absorbs water, weighs more and does not perform as intended.

When you begin casting, select a spot where you want your fly to land. This should be a foot or two ahead of any fish because if you land a fly directly on top of the fish, it may ignore the fly. Trout want to see the fly floating toward them in a feeding lane that is normally slightly off to their side.

After you cast the fly the correct distance, gently lower your rod tip and the line and fly will drop to the water. You want this drop to be gentle and you'll see a "U" unfold and the line will extend out in front with the fly. Any erratic and forceful drops that make a splash will alert a trout to your presence and can turn off their intentions of feeding. Cast forcefully but land gently.

It's important to pay attention to all of the line that is extended beyond

your fly rod tip. Eddies can cause some of the line that is resting on the water surface to float upstream and rushing waters can cause line to be dragged downstream. This puts pressure on your fly line and causes it to tow or drag the fly across the water surface in an unnatural manner. If you see a dry fly dive or move with a V-wake behind it, you need to take action. It is time to mend the line.

To mend, lift the rod tip and flip the fly line in a small or large arch—depending upon water force and how much line you have extended—until the fly is again floating calmly. You might have to mend constantly in rapidly flowing water or skip it all together in other areas. Let the fly and line tell you when it's time to mend. For a beginner, you might find the parachute dry fly patterns with the extended bright yellow or glowing white yarns easier to follow. You can also keep track of your fly by watching the end of your fly line. It frequently points to the fly's location.

You can often get a dry fly to dance by slightly twitching the tip of your fly rod. This will place coils and pressure in the line and

TIP:

Wade Wisely
Be careful when you wade, you might be alerting fish to your presence. Odors from food, tobacco, and other sources that may be on your waders and hands can disperse over a wide area—and detected by sensitive trout—when you enter the water. The same is true of walking rapidly and tumbling rocks.

Fish facing upstream and you'll come in behind a trout without spooking it if all goes as planned.

If you need to cast downstream, use a parachute or stop cast to keep the fly from dragging when it hits the water.

TIP:

False Casting
False casting is casting without dropping the fly onto or into the water. You could be trying to gain distance or change directions and a false cast lets you line up your fly with the rod. False casting can also be used to dry a wet dry fly and make it more buoyant.

push—or pull—the line, leader, tippet and ultimately the fly. With a little practice and under the right water conditions, you can almost make the fly spin in a full circle.

This practice is best mastered on a lake or pond where you can clearly observe the line and the fly. Water grips the fly not unlike grass, and you need to determine how much pressure you must apply to make your rod and fly line spring to action. Each rig reacts differently and this is a technique that can take practice and time to master. When you can make your dry fly dance on the surface, you've opened a new door to fly-fishing enjoyment.

Retrieve excess fly line with your noncasting hand—left in the illustration above—as the fly and fly line are being pushed downstream toward you by the current. You

want to be able to lift the rod and tip to quickly set the hook when a trout grabs your fly. Slack line will permit enough time for the trout to reject your fly when it discovers that it's not the real thing. A major reason that fly anglers miss their fish is because they cannot apply sufficient pressure to the hook to set it in the fish's mouth. Keeping a line semi-tight and ready for action will prevent this.

After the fly line and fly has washed past you, it's time to cast again. If you need to reduce the amount of line that you have extended, now is a good time to wind some back onto the reel. As you cast, you can control or increase your line by pulling or holding the line securely with your noncasting hand.

Take note that if the fish seem to

be extra spooky where you are fishing—often the result of too much fishing pressure—the trout may become sensitive to the sound of fine drops of moisture falling on the surface. Avoid this splash by false casting over land or away from the area where you intend to finally place your fly.

While casting and fishing you should pause to remove algae, weeds and other debris from your line. These can greatly reduce your casting ability and the performance of your line. This is a good opportunity to check for wind knots and inspect any knots that you tied as you assembled the leader, tippet and fly.

Casting and fishing with dry flies is popular because most anglers can easily see the fly floating and bobbing in the current and see a trout dash up and grab the fly. Remember, however, that nearly 90 percent of the time a fish spends feeding is done subsurface. To pick up more fish, you'll have to explore the underwater world where they lurk. This takes practice, time and mastering of a few basic skills.

and is being naturally swept along by the current. Any fish that spots a fly washing through its feeding line will be enticed to strike the fly.

Questions, however, do arise. How deep is that pool or what is the depth of the bottom of the river? How do you get a fly down to the right depth? Since you cannot see down there, how do you know what's happening in the depths? How do you tell when a fish has the fly? These are all good questions that are simple to answer. Most involve keenly observing your line and feeling with your fly rod. Here's where spending money for a quality rod that's sensitive will offer rewards. While top-quality rods might seem flimsy, this often translates into sensitive. If you hold the rod properly, with your thumb on top of the cork grip, you can often feel your fly bumping the bottom or will notice a slight twitch or vibration in the line when a fish has grabbed hold. This is a skill that improves with time. The more times that you go fishing to increase your experience and knowledge, the better the angler you will become.

WOOLLY WORM

(Wet Fly)
Popular Sizes:
06, 08, 10, 12
Additional Colors:
Black, brown, olive
Hook Type:
3X long nymph
Thread:
Black 6/0
Tail:
Red hackle fibers
Body:
Black, olive, or brown chenille
Hackle:
Badger or grizzly, palmered over body.

Nymphing

This tactic involves placing a fly at a desired depth to attract the attention of a trout. The object is to make the nymph bounce along on the bottom of the river, stream or lake and look as if it were knocked free or dislodged from a boulder

Water Depth

Water quality can lead to misconceptions about water depth. Trout streams can be ribbons of gin clear water rushing through scenic countryside. A pool of water that appears to be a few feet deep has caught many anglers by surprise

Casting is done with the right hand while controlling the line with the left. This can be reversed in the case of "lefties."

TIP:

Be Alert

Hungry trout will sometimes mistake a strike indicator for a fly and will dash up to take a better look or actually grab the indicator. If this happens, pass your nymph through the area where the trout came from.

when the bottom was actually farther down than the angler was tall. Tread with caution to avoid taking an unwanted or embarrassing plunge into the depths.

One way to determine depth is to wade into a hole and do some exploring. Obviously, after you have waded through a pool will not be the best time to flyfish it because you have alerted the trout. The information garnered, however, will help you determine how deep the water is and how far down you can see. Normally a pool more than three feet deep will not have vegetation growing in its depths. A wading staff is helpful in your exploration.

I've witnessed anglers tossing stones and small boulders into pools to try and determine how deep they were or to chase fish out. You can forget trying to catch any fish that's treated to this punishment, and the chances are good that every fish in nearby water has been alerted by the vibrations, thuds and echoes of rocks hitting the bottom or making a resounding splash.

Go Deep

Once you determine how deep a pool of water is—or appears to be—you want to get your nymph, wet fly or streamer down where the trout are. Weight is the answer.

Weighted nymphs are the best bet. These heavier flies will become snagged less than weights and will still appear lifelike to a trout. The weight is often a metal bead, a wrap of lead or other material that is built into the fly.

To add more weight as needed, there are split shot, putty, wraps and other options. Each of these adds weight near the fly to pull it down deep into the water. Most weights are attached at a minimum of 8 to 12 inches ahead of the fly. This permits the fly to wash along freely and appear more lifelike. Sometimes the weight can be added by a small section of tippet that is tied onto your leader. The tippet with its weighty load can slide up and down the line as needed. If this rig becomes snagged, you can also tug until the weights slip off the end of the line to set you free. This avoids losing line and a fly.

Reading the Action

Once you have a nymph or fly working along in the depths of a pool or river, how can you tell what is going on down there? Vibration and sensing action through your fly rod and line are the first steps. You'll often feel the slight shake.

Watching the line can also reveal clues. If a trout moves into a feeding lane, grabs your fly, and then moves back to its holding area, you can often spot this. You'll see your line or leader move upstream or off to the side from the direction it was traveling. It pays to be keenly observant.

Another option is adding strike indicators. These are often small pieces of foam with one side pre-coated with adhesive. You simply remove the indicator from its card or paper base, wrap it around the leader or tippet and stick it together. Other strike indicators include round foam mini balls that are held in place with plugs or toothpick sections and fuzzy yarn indicators that are easily looped into the leader or tippet. Another popular option—where legal—is to tie on a dry fly, then tie the section of tippet and your nymph into the bend of the dry fly hook. You can fish the water with a dry and wet fly and gain the attention of more fish.

You have to be observant when fishing with a nymph. Watch the strike indicator for any erratic behavior, including a sudden stop. If the indicator moves to the side or stops, the chances are that your nymph or fly has stopped moving underneath the surface. If the indicator moves upstream rapidly, raise your fly rod and set the hook. If it has paused,

you can begin lifting the fly rod tip and try to detect vibration that will reveal a trout. If the fly seems to be captured by a rock, debris, limbs, etc., try to move the tip of the rod upstream and pull the fly line, leader and the fly back up in the direction from which it came to dislodge it. If you have set the hook and have snagged a limb or weed, you might have to wade out, run your hand down the line and attempt to find and dislodge the fly. This is where a catch-and-release works well. You slide the front opening around the line, move it down the line until it wraps around the fly and then apply pressure to dislodge it. This greatly reduces the chances of impaling your hand with a sharp hook.

Trout like this are the payoff of successful fishing tactics. With practice and experience you can develop your own fishing style to get results.

Fishing Big Flies

Huge flies, like Whitlock's grasshoppers, muddler minnows and streamers present new fly-fishing challenges. These flies are a little more difficult to cast and you'll need to work the rod and fly line differently to make them move naturally while underwater.

Dancing Flies
If you've ever watched a newly hatched fly on the surface of the water, you'll notice that it often dances and buzzes around in erratic circles until lift-off and when it's free of the water's pull. Fish find this movement very attractive.

Most grasshopper patterns and some cricket patterns tied today have foam bodies. They are easy to cast and float high. If you've ever watched a grasshopper in the water, they kick and glide a few inches until they reach shore. You can imitate this kick-and-glide action by giving the fly line a jerk toward you with your line managing hand. Simply tug the line a few inches at a time and the grasshopper should glide a couple of inches across the surface. No need to use any weights or strike indicators that could cause unnatural movement.

Streamers are different. These oftentimes imitate small minnows or long leeches. Leeches wiggle and glide near the bottom of lakes and rivers so the same principle you use for the grasshopper can apply with woolly buggers and other leech imitations. You want the fly to twitch as it moves, and you will need to keep slight pressure on the line.

Streamers that imitate minnows can be fished across a pool or stream with great success. As it passes across the water a fish looking upstream could see this minnow imitation dart by in front—and this is a meal that's often too hard to ignore. Pay close attention and keep the line tight as the fly makes a bend. A fish in the area that thinks the minnow imitation has seen it and is trying to escape will attack the fly with brute predator force—even if it is not hungry!

For large rivers and lakes, you can also fish streamers down current from you. This is one of the few times when I fish downstream and retrieve flies to me. A quick jerk of the line and moving the rod tip from side to side can cause the streamer to imitate an injured minnow and this attracts larger fish.

Go Forth

There are no "must-do" ways to fly fish. Each angler develops his or her own casting and fishing style, and these vary as the angler progresses in experience and changes to meet water conditions. If you are not catching fish, watch other anglers, ask your friends or hire a guide. You'll find a competent guide to be some of the best money you'll spend on a fishing trip because they often know what the local fish like—and don't like.

Selecting the right fly can increase your chances of landing a huge trout.

CRICKET   MINNOW

Stream Etiquette

No book on flyfishing would be complete without mentioning how to be socially responsible while fly-fishing. Use common sense and remember that fishing is supposed to be fun, not a competitive sport.

If someone is fishing a pool or stretch on a river, do not cut them off. Nothing riles a person faster than having someone step into the head of the pool they are fishing. When in doubt of how much room to give an angler before you start fishing, move at least 100 yards farther upriver or ask the anglers what their intentions are and how far they plan to fish. A little politeness goes a long way.

Drift boats, pontoons, canoes, etc., are the vehicles and rivers are the highways when you're fishing. Therefore, any angler wading in the water should be given wide berth. Pedestrians have the right of way on land—and in the water.

Always try to leave a stream, lake or river in better shape than you find it. Try picking up garbage at the trailhead or improving a section of the path. If a place looks well taken care of, others might treat the place with more respect.

Be socially responsible and contact elected officials and speak up on behalf of trout and natural resources when you hear that "new highway development" or other construction will imperil the local trout population. When "progress" destroys the quality of life for trout, fly anglers everywhere will have their quality of life eroded in multiple factors.

Be a good water steward and be kind to fellow anglers. The rewards will come your way.

Use a tight casting loop and false casting to increase distance and change direction.

Appendix: *State Fish Departments*

These addresses and contact details should be a first stop when you seek places to fly fish. Many agencies offer free booklets with maps and other details about trout seasons and requirements.

Alabama Division of Wildlife and Freshwater Fisheries
64 N. Union Street
Montgomery, AL 36130
(334) 242-3465
http://www.dcnr.state.al.us/agfd/email.html

Alaska Department of Fish and Game
P.O. Box 25526
Juneau, Alaska 99802-5526
(907) 465-4100
http://www.state.ak.us/local/akpages/FISH.GAME/adfghome.htm

Arizona Game and Fish Department
2221 W. Greenway Rd.
Phoenix, Arizona 85023-4399
(602) 942-3000
http://www.gf.state.az.us/frames/index.html

Arkansas Game & Fish Commission
#2 Natural Resources Dr.
Little Rock, Arkansas 72205
(800) 364-GAME
http://www.agfc.com

California Department of Fish and Game
1416 9th Street
Sacramento, CA 95814
(916) 653 - 7664
http://www.dfg.ca.gov/dfghome.html

Colorado Division of Wildlife
6060 Broadway
Denver, Colorado 80216
(303) 297-1192
http://wildlife.state.co.us/

Connecticut Department of Environmental Protection Wildlife Division
79 Elm Street
Hartford, Connecticut 06106-5127
(860) 424-3011
http://dep.state.ct.us/burnatr/
Email:
webmaster@po.state.ct.us

Georgia Department of Natural Resources
2070 U.S. Hwy. 278, S.E.
Social Circle, GA 30025
(770) 918-6408
http://georgianet.org/dnr/wild/

State of Hawaii, Department of Land and Natural Resources
Kalanimoku Bldg. Rm 130
1151 Punchbowl St.
Honolulu, HI 96813
Phone: (808)587-0400
http://www.state.hi.us/dlnr/
dlnr@exec.state.hi.us

Idaho Fish and Game
P.O. Box 25
Boise, Idaho 83707
http://www2.state.id.us/fishgame/idfginfo@idfg.state.id.us

Illinois DNR Division of Wildlife Resources
One Natural Resources Way
Springfield, IL 62702-1271
(217) 782-6302
http://dnr.state.il.us/PIO@dnrmail.state.il.us

Indiana Division of Fish and Wildlife
402 W. Washington St.
Room W273
Indianapolis, Indiana 46204
(317) 232-4080
http://www.state.in.us/dnr/fishwild/index.htm

Iowa Fish and Wildlife Division
Henry A. Wallace Building
900 E. Grand
Des Moines, IA 50319-0034
(515) 281-4687
http://www.state.ia.us/dnr/fwdiv.htm

Kentucky Department of Fish and Wildlife
#1 Game Farm Road
Frankfort, Kentucky 40601
(800) 858-1549
http://www.kdfwr.state.ky.us/
info.center@mail.state.ky.us

Maine Department of Inland Fisheries and Wildlife
284 State Street
41 State House Station
Augusta, Maine 04333-0041
(207) 287-8000
http://www.state.me.us/ifw/index.htm

Massachusetts Division of Fish & Wildlife
100 Combridge Street Rm. 1902
Boston, MA 02202
(617) 727-3151
http://www.state.ma.us/dfwele/dfw/
Mass.Wildlife@state.ma.us

Michigan Department of Natural Resources
Stevens T. Mason Building
530 W. Allegan St.
P.O. Box 30028
Lansing, Michigan 48909
(517) 373-2329
http://www.michigan.gov/dnr

Minnesota Department of Natural Resources
500 Lafayette Road
St. Paul, MN 55155-4040
(651) 297-1308
http://www.dnr.state.mn.us/
info@dnr.state.mn.us

Missouri Department of Conservation
Administrative Office
P.O. Box 180 (zip 65102)
2901 W. Truman Blvd.
Jefferson City, MO 65109
573/751-4115
Fax: 573/751-4467
http://www.conservation.state.mo.us/fish/

Montana Fish, Wildlife and Parks
1420 East Sixth Ave.
P.O. Box 200701
Helena, Montana 59620
(406) 444-2535
http://www.fwp.state.mt.us/
fwpgen@state.mt.us

Nebraska Game and Parks Commission
2200 N. 33rd St.
Lincoln, Nebraska 68503
(402) 471-0641
http://www.ngpc.state.ne.us/homepage.html

Nevada Division of Wildlife
P.O. Box 10678
1100 Valley Road
Reno, Nevada 89520
(775) 688-1500
http://www.nevadadivisionofwildlife.org/
Email:
ndowinfo@govmail.state.nv.us

New Hampshire Fish and Game Department
2 Hazen Drive
Concord, NH 03301
(603) 271-3211
http://www.wildlife.state.nh.us/
info@wildlife.state.nh.us

New Jersey Division of Fish Wildlife
P.O. Box 400
Trenton, New Jersey 08625-0400
(609)292-2965
http://www.state.nj.us/dep/fgw/

New Mexico Department of Game and Fish
P.O. Box 25112
Sante Fe, New Mexico 87504
http://www.gmfsh.state.nm.us/
web_adm@gmfsh.state.nm.us

New York Division of Fish, Wildlife, and Marine Resources
50 Wolf Road
Albany, New York 12233-4750
(518) 457-5690
http://www.dec.state.ny.us/website/dfwmr/index.html

North Carolina Wildlife Resources Commission
512 N. Salisbury St.
Raleigh, North Carolina 27604-1188
(919) 733-3391
http://www.wildlife.state.nc.us/

North Dakota Game & Fish Dept.
100 N. Bismarck Expressway
Bismarck, North Dakota 58501-5095
General Info: (701) 328-6300
Licensing: (701) 328-6335
Instant Licensing: (800) 406-6409
Hunter Ed: (701) 328-6312
ndgf@state.nd.us
http://www.state.nd.us/gnf/index.html

Ohio Department of Natural Resources
Division of Wildlife
1840 Belcher Dr.
Columbus, Ohio 43224-1329
(614)265-6300
http://www.dnr.state.oh.us/wildlife/default.htm

Oklahoma Department of Wildlife Conservation
1801 N. Lincoln
Oklahoma City, Oklahoma 73105
http://www.wildlifedepartment.com/
pmoore@odwc.state.ok.us

Oregon Department of Fish and Wildlife
ODFW Information
PO Box 59
Portland, Oregon 97207
http://www.dfw.state.or.us/
odfw.Info@state.or.us

Pennsylvania Fish and Boat Commision
3532 Walnut Street
Harrisburg, PA 17109-3618
(717) 787-4250
http://www.pgc.state.pa.us/
info@pgc.state.pa.us
http://www.fish.state.pa.us/

Rhode Island Division of Fish & Wildlife
4808 Tower Hill Road
Wakefield, RI 02879
(401) 789-3094
http://www.state.ri.us/dem/programs/bnatres/fishwild/index.htm

South Carolina Department of Natural Resources
1000 Assembly Street
Columbia, South Carolina 29201
(803) 734-3888
http://water.dnr.state.sc.us/

South Dakota Department of Game, Fish & Parks
(605) 773-3485
http://www.state.sd.us/gfp/
Wildinfo@gfp.state.sd.us

Tennessee Wildlife Resource Agency
Ellington Agricultural Center
P.O. Box 40747
Nashville, Tennessee 37204
(615) 781-6552
http://www.state.tn.us/twra/
cfreeman2@mail.state.tn.us

Texas Parks and Wildlife
4200 Smith School Road
Austin, Texas 78744
http://www.tpwd.state.tx.us/

Utah Division of Wildlife Resources
Box 146301
Salt Lake City, Utah 84114-6301
http://www.wildlife.utah.gov/nrdwr.sfo
wlks@state.ut.us

Vermont Fish and Wildlife
10 South - 103 South Main St.
Waterbury, Vermont 05671-0501
(802)241-3701
http://www.anr.state.vt.us/fw/fwhome/index.htm
jhall@fpr.anr.state.vt.us

Virginia Department of Game and Inland Fisheries
4010 West Broad Street
Richmond, Virginia 23230
(804) 367-1000
http://www.dgif.state.va.us/dgifweb@dgif.state.va.us

Washington Department of Fish & Wildlife
600 Capitol Way N.
Olympia, Washington 98501-1091
(360) 902-2200
http://www.wa.gov/wdfw/home.htm

West Virginia Department of Natural Resources
State Capital Complex, Build. 3
1900 Kanawha Blvd., East
Charleston, WV 25305-0060
(304) 558-3399
http://www.dnr.state.wv.us/
wildlife@dnr.state.wv.us

Wisconsin Department of Natural Resources
101 S Webster St
PO Box 7921
Madison Wisconsin
53707-7921
http://www.dnr.state.wi.us/

Wyoming Fish & Game Dept.
5400 Bishop Boulevard
Cheyenne, Wyoming 82006
(307) 777-4600
http://gf.state.wy.us/
bkisse@missc.state.wy.us

Government of the Northwest Territories
Communications Division - Department of the Executive
Box 1320
Yellowknife NT X1A 2L9
Canada
PH: (867) 873-7817
FAX: (867) 873-0104

Index:

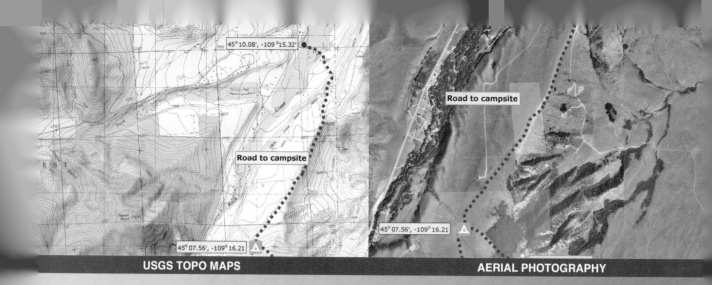